This is a delightfully accessible and refreshingly practical guide to prayer, drawing on a broad range of traditions. Amy's love for the Lord, and her hard-won experience, shines through every page.

PETE GREIG, author of *How to Pray*

Whether your prayer life is vibrant or ho-hum, *7 Ways to Pray* will draw you deeper into the conversation with God you've always longed for. Here you'll find a path forward to the *adventure* that prayer is meant to be!

ELISA MORGAN, speaker, author, cohost of *Discover the Word*

What a beautiful, powerful, and personal journey into God's sustaining presence with the loving and sure-handed guide Amy Boucher Pye. A gentle leader and strong companion, she taps into her uncanny ability to make prayer seem both practical and divine, offering fresh and intentional ways to pray—just when we and our hurting world need prayer the most. This will prove a well-loved classic.

PATRICIA RAYBON, author of *I Told the Mountain to Move*

We're tempted to think of prayer as something that, while it might be essential in some abstract way, exists at the periphery of "real life." Amy Boucher Pye insists that prayer carries us into the heart of what it means to be human, into the center of pulsing life. Prayer carries us

into God's expansive world. If we want to be awakened to what is real, if we want to see with the eyes of faith, then we want to learn to pray. And Amy offers us wonderful guidance.

WINN COLLIER, pastor; author of five books, including *A Burning in My Bones*; director of the Eugene Peterson Center for Christian Imagination

Meister Eckhart, the medieval mystic, summarized prayer by saying, "If the only prayer you ever say in your whole life is 'thank you,' that would suffice." Prayer easily becomes a burden for the disciple, when in fact it offers a path into God's presence, a space free from anxiety. Amy helpfully invites us to explore approaches to prayer where we find rest for our soul.

MICHA JAZZ, head of Waverley Abbey Resources, guardian of St. Cuthbert's Oratory

I once read a book on prayer by a well-known author. It was, as I expected, brilliant. But afterward I noticed something: While reading it, I hadn't actually been moved to pray. Not so with this winsome, practical book by Amy Boucher Pye. *7 Ways to Pray* not only stirred in me a hunger to know God more; it offered creative and accessible ways to do so. Keep this book close by. You'll be returning to it again and again. Highly recommended.

SHERIDAN VOYSEY, author of *The Making of Us, Resurrection Year*, and *Reflect with Sheridan*

What a wonderful, inspirational, and much-needed book! *7 Ways to Pray* brings ancient prayer patterns and practices bang up-to-date, making them meaningful and applicable in wonderfully new ways. I can't wait to use this book regularly as a rich but practical companion to prayer—it really is a gift to Christians everywhere.

CATHY MADAVAN, speaker, writer, broadcaster, author of *Irrepressible*

Amy writes with honesty and wisdom from profound experience and learning. Her book is refreshingly practical and accessible for anyone who wants to grow in prayer, and the ways of praying she explores are an invitation to deep encounter and intimacy with God.

SEAN DOHERTY, principal of Trinity College Bristol

I know few people who find prayer easy, which is why *7 Ways to Pray* will meet such a great need. It is a practical, easy-to-follow guide to the life of prayer. Full of personal stories from the author and examples from church history, this book will help kick-start your prayer life and revitalize your walk with God.

TONY HORSFALL, author, retreat leader, mentor

Amy has written about tried-and-tested techniques of praying in a fresh and accessible way for a new generation. Each of the seven ways is rooted in stories and offers very practical suggestions to get you praying.

LIZ HOARE, author, tutor of spiritual formation at Wycliffe Hall in Oxford

Prayer is communication with God about what we're doing together. No other book offers so many rich and practical ways to go deeper with him. I wish I had discovered *7 Ways to Pray* years ago, and I will be keeping my copy close to me in the future.

JAMES CATFORD, chair of Renovaré

7
WAYS
to
PRAY

Time-Tested
Practices
for Encountering
God

AMY BOUCHER PYE

NavPress ®

*A NavPress resource published in alliance
with Tyndale House Publishers*

NavPress is the publishing ministry of The Navigators, an international Christian organization and leader in personal spiritual development. NavPress is committed to helping people grow spiritually and enjoy lives of meaning and hope through personal and group resources that are biblically rooted, culturally relevant, and highly practical.

For more information, visit NavPress.com.

7 Ways to Pray: Time-Tested Practices for Encountering God

Copyright © 2021 by Amy Boucher Pye. All rights reserved.

A NavPress resource published in alliance with Tyndale House Publishers

NAVPRESS and the NavPress logo are registered trademarks of NavPress, The Navigators, Colorado Springs, CO. *TYNDALE* is a registered trademark of Tyndale House Ministries. Absence of ® in connection with marks of NavPress or other parties does not indicate an absence of registration of those marks.

The Team:
David Zimmerman, Acquisitions Editor; Jennifer Lonas, Copy Editor; Olivia Eldredge, Operations Manager; Ron C. Kaufmann, Designer

Cover photograph of vine by Ergita Sela on Unsplash.

Back cover photograph of ivy copyright © firefox/Depositphotos.com. All rights reserved.

Author photo taken by Donna Ford, copyright © 2020. All rights reserved.

Some of the anecdotal illustrations in this book are true to life and are included with the permission of the persons involved. All other illustrations are composites of real situations, and any resemblance to people living or dead is purely coincidental.

For information about special discounts for bulk purchases, please contact Tyndale House Publishers at csresponse@tyndale.com, or call 1-855-277-9400.

ISBN 978-1-64158-377-0

Printed in the United States of America

27	26	25	24	23	22	21
7	6	5	4	3	2	1

To Nicholas,
who prays faithfully even in the fog,
and to J and A
with hope, faith, and love.
And to those who pray for me—
you know who you are.
I'm forever grateful.

CONTENTS

Foreword

ON THE WALL IN OUR KITCHEN hangs a chalkboard with these words in my handwriting: "Prayer is about being deeply loved."

When I bought the chalkboard shortly after we moved to Michigan in 2003, I intended to use it for a weekly rotation of inspirational quotes. But after a few weeks of those particular words remaining on it, our observant eight-year-old son confronted me. "Mommy, when are you going to change the board?"

Without thinking too deeply about my answer, I replied, "When those words sink into me."

I don't remember how those six words found me. Perhaps it was my own interpretation of something I heard or read. But eighteen years after I first scrawled them in chalk, they serve as both a testimony to God's faithful work of transformation and a reminder of his ongoing invitation: "As the Father has loved me, so I have loved you; abide in my love" (John 15:9, NRSV).

This is prayer: a response of loving attention to the God who loved us first. Prayer is our consent to being loved in the same way that the Father has loved the Son. Prayer is saying yes to the generous hospitality of the God who says to his children, "I have loved you with an everlasting and steadfast love. Remain in my love. Dwell in it. Rest in it. Make yourselves at home in it."

I haven't always seen prayer this way. For many years as a Christian, my prayers were driven by a sense of obligation, duty, fear, and guilt. I was a striver who tried to "do things right" for the Lord. Yes, prayer was a conversation, but that conversation—often an anxious one—began with me and my words to him. By God's grace I began to see a different way, that prayer is not a "method" or "technique" but includes myriad and life-giving ways to practice receiving, resting in, and then responding to the love of God.

Amy Boucher Pye knows this way of prayer and is a trustworthy companion for the journey. With engaging storytelling and practical examples, Amy weaves and translates wisdom from the ancient church into a guidebook that is honest, fresh, and creative. Reading her words is like traveling through a landscape you thought you knew, only to discover treasures you hadn't yet perceived. Even if you are already familiar with some of the prayer practices she describes, you'll find new ways to rest in the love of God. What Amy offers in these pages isn't simply seven ways to pray. These are seven kinds of prayer with many ways to say yes to God's call to deeper intimacy with him.

In other words, you'll find in Amy's beautiful book many ways to say to the Lord, "I love you too."

Grace in the journey,

Sharon Garlough Brown

Introduction

IN MY TWENTIES, my world changed. When I ended a relationship that I thought held my future, I felt bereft and lost. *Who will love me now?* I wondered through my tears. *And now I don't have any friends*, I moaned, thinking of how I'd left my high-school and university friends in Minnesota for the excitement of living in the nation's capital, surrounding myself with those who knew my ex-fiancé.

In my pain, I turned to God. *Are you there?* I cried. *I can't hear you.* More silence. More tears.

Over the next months, in great need, I returned to God again and again, not knowing where else to go. And as the weeks passed, something changed. Through the help of the Holy Spirit, I started to quiet my inner voices—those saying I was worthless and hopeless—as I asked God to meet me. I read the Bible, searching for God as I hungered for love. As he responded, I felt at times as if the words jumped off the page and into my heart. My desire to know God and experience his love fueled my reading, and I woke up earlier and earlier so I could feast on his Word.

I started to copy down passages from the Bible, applying the promises to my life. Although I read without much reference to their original context, I felt God speaking through them to my hurting, yearning heart. For instance, I read Isaiah 43:1-2 and reveled in the words, adapting them as if God were whispering them to me: "Don't be afraid, Amy, for I've saved you. You're passing through the waters, but don't be afraid, for I am with you. The rivers won't sweep over you, for I am the Lord your God." When I reached verse 4, I wondered at the amazing promise of God: "You're precious and honored in my sight. And I love you."

Lord, you love me? I asked. *Do you really love me? Is this promise meant for me?*

As I paused, I sensed a nudge in my spirit, with a resounding *Yes*.

I thought, *Well, it's right there written in the Bible that God loves his people. He must really love me, too.*

As I read each day from the Scriptures and poured out my feelings to God, I started to understand in a new way that I was made in his image and worth loving. I came to believe that these nudges of grace were loving assurances from God. Through my new way of hearing God through his Word, I was changed forever.

The Joys and Challenges of Prayer

That's why I'm so excited about prayer. The Creator of the universe, who is beyond and above us, yearns for a relationship with us. He loves to communicate with us. He receives our longings and our praise, our petitions and our thanks to him. Not only does he respond to the cries of our hearts and the offhand prayers we utter, but he changes us. He makes us more like himself through the working of the Holy Spirit in our lives, and we become more compassionate and caring, more self-controlled and outward looking, wiser and with greater understanding.

But prayer can be hard, too. We might not sense God's presence in our daily lives, or we become disappointed with the circumstances we face. We might feel that God has let us down and wonder if he really is good and loving. Or we might find ourselves in a rut, checking off a daily time of devotions as a duty, not a joy, while uttering a quick prayer before moving on to something seemingly more pressing. How, then, can we reignite our first love? How can we not only enjoy our communication with God but allow him to change us too?

The good news is that God partners with us, meeting us where we're at and helping us communicate with him. That you've picked up this book on prayer indicates your desire to grow closer to God; he'll take that desire and magnify it, even as a mustard seed grows into a big tree. Know that you're not doing this on your own.

Know, too, that God will help you build healthy prayer habits into your life. Although habits don't ensure that we'll automatically respond prayerfully to situations of stress, anxiety, or even positive happenings, they increase the likelihood that we will.

Maybe, though, you'd find it helpful to redefine how you see prayer. We can easily think we've failed if each morning we don't study the Bible and pray. I'm not knocking that kind of committed devotion, but I wouldn't want that practice to be my only way of praying.

You might wonder if God is really there or your prayers are "working" if you don't encounter God in some way—such as through a mighty mystical experience—as you pray. It's true that God sometimes meets us in amazing ways; we may feel cushioned by his love or have a sense of unseen realities being revealed to us. But the wisdom of Christians throughout the centuries, including those seen as mystics, is that these transcendent experiences are neither the norm in the everyday lives of followers of Christ nor the goal of those seeking to communicate with him. For if we view prayer as a portal to some mystical plane, we can turn the act of praying into something we find intimidating, disappointing, or exclusionary of others.

God loves you dearly and yearns to meet with you. He might have a specific gift to impart to you, but he might just want to spend time with you. I'm reminded of Dan Rather's interview with Mother Teresa, when the newscaster asked her what she said during her prayers. She responded, "I listen."

Rather asked, "What does God say to you?"

She said, "He listens."[1]

Ways to Pray

In our journey together, I'll introduce you to some tried and tested ways to pray that you may—or may not—be familiar with. If you feel overwhelmed by the wealth of richness to explore, just focus on one or two of the practices. I hope you can embrace a sense of freedom and fun in using this book, whether moving through it from front to back or jumping from one chapter to another.

You might think of prayer as a solitary activity, but through communal prayer, God can meet us powerfully, whether we come together in pairs, triplets, or in a bigger gathering. You can do many of the prayer exercises in this book on your own, but some are designed for groups as well. You're invited to make up to ten copies of these group exercises without requiring permission.

On this journey together, we'll experience praying with and through the Bible, practicing God's presence, hearing God, praying through lament, praying imaginatively, and praying the examen. These practices have been around for centuries in various forms, but they are as relevant today as when people first used them to encounter our living God— the Trinity of God the Father, God the Son, and God the Holy Spirit.

First we'll look at ways of praying with the Bible, not only using God's Word as a springboard for our prayers, but also as a way to pray that was birthed in the monasteries, *lectio divina* (that's Latin for "sacred reading"). This kind of praying, with its fourfold process of engaging with a scriptural text, helps us slow down to receive from God as we read his Word.

We'll also explore how to practice the presence of God,

acknowledging that he is always with us through the indwelling presence of the Holy Spirit. Brother Lawrence, a monk in France in the seventeenth century, devised a way of praying at all times, but this exercise goes back much further. For instance, John Cassian in the fifth century was keen that the monks under his care should pray unceasingly.

What about hearing God? We'll explore this topic next, examining how people in the Bible heard God's voice. An important part of listening is discernment—testing what we hear to evaluate if we're really hearing God. We'll look at Teresa of Ávila, who lived in Spain in the 1500s—a time of suspicion and fear regarding spiritual matters—to see how she learned to discern God's voice.

Living in a fallen world, we face pain, heartache, and disappointment. We need to know how to lament—to let out feelings of sadness and despair to our heavenly Father. We'll discover the biblical roots of this practice, especially through the Psalms and Lamentations.

We'll continue by engaging prayerfully with the Bible through entering the biblical stories imaginatively. Ignatius of Loyola in sixteenth-century Spain popularized this practice, which can help us move from an overintellectualized reading of the Bible to one that engages our emotions, too.

Looking back can help us move forward through prayerfully examining ourselves with the help of the Holy Spirit. One form of this type of prayer is the examen, which was made popular by Ignatius of Loyola. We'll conclude with his instruction to not only consider the events of the day but also how we respond and see God at work.

A key part of each chapter is the prayer exercises I include. My hope and prayer is that you'll not just read about these ways to pray, but that you'll also put them into practice and encounter our loving God. If you come into his presence and receive from him, I'll give thanks and rejoice.

Are you ready?

Father, Son, and Holy Spirit, open my heart and my mind to receive you during this journey of prayer. Teach me from your well of wisdom as I drink deeply at the source. Strengthen my ability to discern your truth as you drench me with your love and compassion. Amen.

1

GOD'S WORD TO US

How to Pray with the Bible

REJECTED, a thirteen-year-old sobbed into her sleeping bag at summer camp. The start of a teen romantic comedy? Perhaps, but that episode marked the first time I sensed God's voice through his Word.

When we arrived at the camp, we were bowled over by the ratio of boys to girls—just us four girls to twenty guys. We scoped out the guys and giggled over which was the cutest while we canoed in the crystal-clear lakes, cooked over a campfire, swatted mosquitoes, and sang worship songs under the stars.

In the guy department, I kept hoping I'd be chosen, but while each of my three friends paired off, I remained alone.

On the last night, I looked from one friend to the next, each of whom was holding hands or standing arm in arm with their guys around the campfire.

Then one of the nonattached guys sneered at me. He pointed to an overweight boy and then to me (I was not thin) and said, "Oh, why don't *you two* get together?"

Mortified, I ran back to my tent, scurried into my sleeping bag, and released my sobs, feeling undesirable and worthless. Our camp counselor came and tried to comfort me, but I pretended to be asleep. A few minutes later, she left.

When at last the week was over and I was back at home, I tried to forget my feelings of rejection. I put on a brave face and pushed my hurt into a corner, not wanting to share it with my parents or friends. Or with God.

But to my surprise I received a letter from my camp counselor, who said how concerned she had been for me. The verses she quoted from Philippians pierced through my hardened exterior:

> I thank my God every time I remember you. In all
> my prayers for all of you, I always pray with joy . . .
> being confident of this, that he who began a good
> work in you will carry it on to completion until the
> day of Christ Jesus. . . .
>
> And this is my prayer: that your love may
> abound more and more in knowledge and depth
> of insight, so that you may be able to discern what
> is best and may be pure and blameless for the day

of Christ, filled with the fruit of righteousness that comes through Jesus Christ—to the glory and praise of God.[1]

I ran down to my room, found my Bible, and looked for Philippians, reading the whole passage more than once. For the first time I felt as if God was speaking to me through the Scriptures. The words sailed off the page and landed in my heart, penetrating the places of hurt and rejection. I started to believe that the Lord had started a good work in me and that he wouldn't leave me. That I'd grow in wisdom and insights and would bear fruit. With the pages blurry through my tears, I pondered the promises in Paul's letter and began to make them my own.

That camp counselor was a conduit of God's grace, pointing me to his words of transforming love. I had begun the exhilarating journey of meeting God as I prayed and read his Word.

The Knowable God

God always makes himself known to us, and a primary way he reveals himself is through his Word. When we pray with the Bible, God infuses the experience with his Spirit. As with my memorable encounter after camp, God comforts us through what we read. Sometimes he corrects us or convicts us; often he teaches us as he imparts his wisdom.

The Bible's story of God and his people is one of intimacy and communication. It started when God spoke to Adam and Eve directly in the Garden as he delighted in them and instructed them. When sin marred the relationship between him and his people, he called them back to himself, speaking to the Israelites through the prophets by the inspiration of the Spirit. Later, God the Father sent Jesus the Son to be "the Word [who] was with God, and . . . was God."[2] God then sent us the Holy Spirit to dwell with us and in us as he comforts and teaches us. The unreachable, unknowable God reaches down and makes himself known.

God, as Father, Son, and Holy Spirit, has also given us the Bible, limiting his words to a level we can understand. Thus, the church fathers spoke of the Bible as the "abbreviated word."[3] God our Creator meets us with grace and love in a form we can grasp. Jesus the Word fills the pages of Scripture with his acts of grace and redemption. And just as the Holy Spirit breathed the Scripture itself into life, so the Spirit breathes life into us as we read it.

As we pray with the Bible, we welcome God's Word to come and live in us. One of the Puritans, William Law (1686–1761), illustrated this when he said that Scripture "should only be read in an attitude of prayer, trusting to the inward working of the Holy Spirit to make [its truth] a living reality within us."[4]

For many Christians, the first and most common way of engaging with God's Word is with their intellect. This is good—vibrant and strong Bible study is important to sustain a vital faith. But this shouldn't be our only way of reading the Bible. We might think of Martin Luther

(1483–1546) as one who studied the Bible deeply, which he did. But he was also steeped in a prayerful reading of it. He said, "You should meditate . . . not only in your heart, but also externally . . . reading and rereading [the words of Scripture] with diligent attention and reflection, so that you may see what the Holy Spirit means by them."[5] Perhaps Luther drew on his experience as a monk in making this observation, for in the monasteries they spoke Scripture aloud as they prayed.

Take and Eat

"Don't swallow it in a big lump!" That was the warning of the beloved French abbot Bernard of Clairvaux (1090–1153), who delighted in a slow, deliberate reading of the Bible. He said that if we eat too quickly, without careful chewing, we'll be cheated of the delicious flavor of the Bible, which is sweetened by the spice of the Holy Spirit.[6]

This sense of eating the Scriptures—chewing on them, swallowing them, and feeding on them—comes through in the Old Testament. The prophets Ezekiel and Jeremiah ate God's Word and delighted in it. Ezekiel said, "It tasted as sweet as honey in my mouth."[7] For Jeremiah, God's words were his "joy and [his] heart's delight."[8] The image of eating underscores the importance of bringing God's Word deeply inside ourselves. We can chew and meditate on it, receiving its nourishment as it feeds us from the sweetness of God's love.

As we eat God's Word, it makes itself at home within us,

as we see in Paul's letter to the Colossians: We "let the word of Christ dwell in [us] richly."[9] In the Greek this means that God's Word comes and stays in us.[10] First we welcome the Word as a visitor to our dwelling—that is, to our minds and hearts. Then we keep on extending the invitation until the houseguest becomes a permanent resident inside us.

As we dwell in the Word and it lives in us, it comes alive within us, as the writer to the Hebrews said: "The word of God is alive and active. Sharper than any double-edged sword, it penetrates even to dividing soul and spirit, joints and marrow; it judges the thoughts and attitudes of the heart."[11] We can experience those uncanny moments of coming across a passage and feeling the words burn into our hearts. God can comfort us when we're hurting as we read a line of the Psalms; he can convict us with his teaching from the Sermon on the Mount. As you read the Scriptures, pause before you delve into them and ask God to speak to you. He loves to respond when we seek him.

When we consider the charge to take and eat, we can ponder a striking image that church father Origen (c. 184–c. 253) used: "His flesh and blood . . . are the divine Scriptures, eating which, we have Christ; the words becoming his bones, the flesh becoming the meaning from the text . . . and the blood being faith in the gospel of the new covenant."[12]

If you're comfortable doing so, sit with those images of sinew and text for a few minutes, asking God to bring them to life in your mind's eye so that you can grasp in a new way the relationship between Christ and the Scriptures.

Prayer Practices

Following are some ways to pray with the Bible, all of which I've employed during various seasons of my life. As one who enjoys writing, I tend to focus on the practices that involve creating a Scripture poem or putting the text into my own words. You, of course, may resonate with the Bible differently.

Moments of Grace

At times in our journey of faith, we might be tempted to play "Bible roulette," where we open the Bible randomly to find a specific passage meant for us in that moment. But this practice doesn't always have the hoped-for results. When I prepared a talk about praying with the Bible, I decided to open the Bible and see what I landed on. Jeremiah 6:5 made me take pause: "So arise, let us attack at night and destroy her fortresses!"

Yet Francis of Assisi (1181–1226) found his life's calling through a seemingly random act of God. He went over to a prayer book and asked God to guide him. He let the book fall open, and there found his vocation to spend his life for the poor.[13] The early Franciscans followed Francis in this practice, opening the Bible three times when they sought God's guidance.[14]

My dad tells the story of how he and my mom wanted a Scripture passage for each of us children. They prayed and then opened their Bible, and the verses they found for each of us have over the years proven apt. For example, for the child who went through a period of rebellion, they received, "Parents, never drive your children to resentment but bring them up with correction and advice inspired by the Lord."[15] For another child, about whom they prayed for direction and guidance: "Let us never slacken in doing good; for if we do not give up, we shall have our harvest in due time."[16]

I remember a time of deep grief when I opened the Bible in desperation, begging God to speak to me through it. I was nineteen, and I'd just heard the shattering news that one of my closest friends died in a car accident. Plagued with worry about whether she was in heaven, I flipped through my Bible, asking God to show me something—anything—that would help me in my sorrow and confusion. I was amazed to land on this: "The Spirit searches all things, even the deep things of God. For who knows a person's thoughts except their own spirit within them? In the same way no one knows the thoughts of God except the Spirit of God."[17] I read and reread the line from the apostle Paul to the church at Corinth, the words bringing immediate relief. I realized as I digested them that I didn't need to be asking these ultimate questions—I'd never know what went on in Sue's heart and mind. Only she did, and the Spirit of God.

Moments of grace such as these can feel powerful, and undoubtedly God delights in speaking to his children by whatever means we are most open to at a particular moment. But as we mature in our faith, we find that we don't need to search through the Bible randomly. Nor do we view it as a medicine chest, picking out a certain verse in Scripture as a cure for a particular ailment. God wants us to enjoy a relationship of trust with him, where we come to know him intimately through conversation and spending time together. As we seek him and his direction, listening for his leading and obeying him when we sense the way forward, we grow in confidence and in union with him.

I'm not suggesting you play Bible roulette, but perhaps God would delight to impart to you something from his Word; maybe he's waiting for you to take the time to listen and seek him out. Why not spend a few moments resting in God's presence, a Bible open in your lap, or a Bible app open on your phone? Ask God through his Spirit to bring to mind something from his Word just for you, for right now. A well-loved phrase from one of the New Testament letters might pop into your head, or maybe a refrain from a song or hymn based on a passage from the Bible, or even the chapter and verse reference of a Scripture text itself. Wait and receive, and then spend some time weighing how the text applies to your life and whether you've heard from God.

A version of this exercise—one that might appeal especially to extroverts—is to ask God to reveal a passage from the Bible through one of your conversations today. Our Western culture has been soaked in Scripture throughout the centuries, with so many well-known phrases becoming part of common parlance that we might not even be aware of them. Be open and notice God's Spirit at work through the words you speak and hear.

Personalize Scripture

After her beloved dog died, Susan received a visit from her lifelong friend Cheryl, who came to support her as she grieved her sweet canine companion. Susan had prayed for years that Cheryl would come to know Jesus, but Susan had always hesitated to talk about her faith with her. But when they went for a walk in memory of their furry friend, Susan felt moved several times to personalize Scripture, speaking it out to her friend: "For God so loved Cheryl, that he gave his only begotten Son . . ."[18]

Susan later felt God was at work when she read that day's devotional from *Our Daily Bread*, which was an article I'd written titled "Called by Name." I wrote of how Mary Magdalene's attention was arrested when Jesus spoke her name at his tomb, and how God similarly calls us by name.[19] Susan delighted to give Cheryl the article, pointing out how the topic fit so well with their conversation on the walk. She told Cheryl that God cared not only for the big things in her life but also for the little things, because he knew her and called her by name. Susan found her experience of personalizing Scripture for her friend profound and moving, and Cheryl felt that God cared for her.

I, too, have used the act of personalizing Scripture. After a breakup, I needed a practice that wouldn't overwhelm me but would penetrate to the tender places within. I began writing out some of what Jesus said in the gospel stories, adding my name again and again so that the words would move from my head to my heart: "Amy, ask and it will be given to you;

seek and you will find; knock and the door will open."[20] Or, "When you exalt yourself, Amy, you will be humbled, but when you humble yourself, you will be exalted."[21] Or, "Amy, my peace I leave with you; my peace I give you. I do not give to you as the world gives. Amy, do not let your heart be troubled and do not be afraid."[22] Seeing my name in these familiar words helped me realize that God could intend them for me.

I recommend this simple practice, which can have profound results. Wonder where to start? Here are some suggestions, and yes, a few of them cut to the heart:

- Matthew 6:25-34 (Don't worry)
- Matthew 18:6-9 (Causing others to stumble)
- Mark 7:17-23 (That which defiles)
- Mark 13:32-37 (Keeping watch)
- Luke 6:20-26 (Blessings and woes)
- Luke 13:22-30 (The narrow door)
- John 14:15-21 (The promised Holy Spirit)
- John 17:20-26 (Jesus' prayer for us)

Write Bible-Inspired Prayers
I like to give myself permission to put the Bible into my own words. As I write, I ask God to slow me down and help me engage with the meaning. I seek the Holy Spirit to highlight words or phrases that especially resonate with that moment in my life.

One example is Paul's prayer from Ephesians 1:17-19:

I keep asking that the God of our Lord Jesus
Christ, the glorious Father, may give you the Spirit
of wisdom and revelation, so that you may know
him better. I pray that the eyes of your heart may
be enlightened in order that you may know the
hope to which he has called you, the riches of
his glorious inheritance in his holy people, and
his incomparably great power for us who
believe.

We can recast this prayer, while retaining much of the language from our English version:

Glorious God and Father of our Lord Jesus Christ,
I ask that you would give me your Spirit of wisdom
and revelation that I might know you better. Open
the eyes of my heart and enlighten me, that I might
know the hope to which you have called me—
the riches of your glorious inheritance and your
incomparably great power. Amen.

Just a few changes—turning Paul's words into the first-person singular (or plural)—make the prayer feel like it's our own.

Writing out passages of Scripture can move us naturally to pray about concerns in our lives. Here's how I engaged with Jeremiah 46:27 some years ago, first typing out the words of Scripture to let them sink into my heart:

I will surely save you out of a distant place,
    your descendants from the land of their exile.
Jacob will again have peace and security,
    and no one will make him afraid.

From this passage, I wrote a prayer that reflected my own journey:

Lord, you will certainly save us out of a distant place.
Today even after nearly eight years, England feels
like a distant place. Celebrating my son's second
birthday, not with my family of origin, but here in
this distant land. You said to the Israelites long ago
that you would save them from the land of exile.
Well, their descendants, that is. And no one would
make them afraid. Save me, Lord, and make me
not afraid. Give me peace and security, I pray.[23]

Select a passage to engage with; for example, if you're
reading through a book of the Bible, take the next section
you're reading. Put it into your own words, as a prayer of
intercession, a cry of the heart, or a prose rendering. You may
wish to pray through the content and apply it to your life or
to something you're concerned about in the world.

Pen a Scripture Poem

Madame Guyon (1648–1717) wrote, "If you read [Scripture]
quickly, it will benefit you little. You will be like a bee that

merely skims the surface of a flower."[24] Writing down the Scriptures as a prose poem slows down our reading so that we can, in Guyon's words, "plunge deeply within to remove its deepest nectar."[25]

For many years, I've taken the bit of the Bible I'm pondering that day and turned it into a Scripture poem. This practice helps me consider the words and their meaning slowly and meditatively. Through this stripping-down process, I turn the ideas over in my head and my heart.

Here's an example from when Jesus taught his disciples and the crowds, adapted from Luke 6:37-38:

Judge not
and you won't be judged.
Condemn not
and you won't be condemned.
Forgive
and you'll be forgiven.
Give
and you'll receive.

Into your lap
will be poured
a good measure—
pressed down,
shaken together,
and running over.

With the measure you use,
it'll be measured to you.

Writing the words of Scripture in this condensed form helps us get to the heart of the passage. The process of winnowing the words, shaving them down to the few needed to convey the meaning, helps us grasp their wisdom at a deeper level. And it's fun.

꙾

As we pray God's words to us in the Bible, we find Jesus the Word meeting us and the Holy Spirit guiding, comforting, and convicting us. Praying with the Bible provides a foundation for our lives as we follow God, receiving and extending his love. We can enjoy many ways to pray with and through the Bible, including an ancient practice we'll explore next.

2

LECTIO DIVINA

How to Pray through the Bible

WHEN AUTHOR JAMES BRYAN SMITH was at university, his faith came alive, and he devoured the Bible, delving deeply into God's Word through study and worship. Eventually he transferred to a Christian university and then went to seminary—all the time gaining more and more knowledge about the Bible. He even learned Hebrew and Greek, the original languages.

But eventually James's faith started to shrivel up. And his reading of the Bible became a chore instead of a life-giving exercise. In desperation, he agreed to go on a five-day silent retreat at a local monastery. Although he wasn't sure what he would find there, he felt so cut off from God that he was willing to try anything.

As part of the retreat, he met each day with a spiritual director, one of the monks. After James poured out his troubles and how dry he felt spiritually, the monk assigned him the task of slowly reading Luke 1:26-38, where Mary heard from the angel Gabriel that she would be the mother of Jesus. James did so but found it a "boring birth narrative." When the monk asked him to share how he was getting on with this story, James presented scholarly findings. Not impressed, the monk advised him to create some conditions for God to communicate with him through the passage. He said, "When you surrender yourself to the passage, the Spirit will speak."

James returned to his room and tried again, but nothing. Silence.

Broken, he prayed, "God, please speak to me. I am ready to hear whatever you have for me." He read the passage again, and this time the words seemed different—alive and new. He put himself in Mary's place and experienced what she might have felt when the angel spoke to her. The Holy Spirit touched James, and he was able to express some of the fears he had pushed down that bubbled below the surface of his heart. When he thought about Gabriel saying to Mary, "Be not afraid," he, too, sensed God telling him not to fear.

No longer was this book something he only sought to understand with his head, but it became God's love letter to him that reached deeply into his heart. He could now continue studying it while welcoming the Holy Spirit to speak through it, bringing him words of love, affirmation, correction, and comfort.[1]

As James did, so too can we move our reading of the Bible from what may have turned into a dry, rational process to a fresh experience of receiving from God. We can join in praying through the Bible slowly and contemplatively as with expectancy we open ourselves to encounter God.

The Rise and Fall and Rise Again of Sacred Reading

Praying through the Bible has been around for millennia. The Jewish people read the Hebrew Scriptures devotionally, which then influenced the earliest generations of Christians in their approach to the Bible. This way of reading and praying then became a set practice in Christian monasteries when it birthed *lectio divina*, which is the Latin for "sacred reading." This is reading a passage of Scripture several times while chewing on the words and their meaning, being open to the movement of the Holy Spirit while seeking to gain wisdom and grace. This practice gives space for a personal response, such as prayer, praise, and petition. Through it, contemplation of the Word can lead to union with God.

Benedict of Nursia (c. 480–c. 550), often seen as the father of Western monasticism, allocated the best time of the day for sacred reading—up to three hours a day during certain seasons of the year. At that time, with books so rare and precious, reading was a communal activity, not something done on one's own. And because people read aloud, it was a physical practice. Thus, monasteries were called *communities of mumblers*, for monks mouthed the words on which they meditated.[2] One monk was likened to a buzzing bee as he murmured his Psalms.[3]

Spiritual reading became a practice through which God transformed, day by day, those who read the Bible. As they read aloud, they listened for the Voice behind the text, the Author of the Word. They approached their reading with a sense of openness and welcome, not trying to control what would happen.

Developments in culture over the centuries have moved us away from a devotional reading of the Bible. For instance, in the thirteenth century, an emphasis on rationalism started the shift away from the monastic life with its oral culture. The fifteenth century with the invention of the printing press and then the Protestant Reformation in the sixteenth century each contributed to the goal of making the Scriptures available to all, diminishing the communal element of reading the Bible. Then the Enlightenment spurred Protestant scholars to emphasize a historical and critical method of reading Scripture. Each movement, though important, changed the role of sacred reading. Today, however, Christians are returning to ancient practices to experience the presence of God and be made more like him.

A Cord of Four Strands

So what is *lectio divina*, and how do we participate in reading for transformation and encounter with God? This way of heartfelt listening to God is traditionally a circular four-step practice that we undertake with expectancy and awe. In this chapter, we'll explore the steps one by one. But briefly, they are (1) *lectio*, or reading, when we read through the passage with reverence; (2) *meditatio*, reflecting or meditating, when we ruminate over the text as an animal chews its cud; (3) *oratio*, responding or praying, when we voice to God our thanksgiving, praise, petition, repentance, and adoration; and (4) *contemplatio*, resting or contemplating, when we rest in the presence of God. Some people also include a step for pausing at the start, calming ourselves in God's presence, and a step at the end to go forth in action, loving God and his world.

We might, like one of the participants in a talk I gave on *lectio divina*, resist this multistep approach, thinking, *Oh, four steps is a lot!* But as she reflected later, "After doing it, I understood; the more you read a passage, the more it speaks and touches your heart, your need, or your needs of the moment." When we commit time and effort to the process, we put ourselves in a place where God can speak to us.

Michael Casey, a modern-day monk, describes *lectio divina* as akin to "entering a cave."[4] As we start, we need to adjust to the dimmer light. We'll soon come to notice things that were previously hidden to us, perhaps hearing and encountering God in a new way. We'll be molded and changed through these whispers, feelings, songs, and other thoughts that arise in our spirits through the Spirit. We'll receive nourishment for the day—like the Israelites when they ate the daily manna in the desert.

The four stages of sacred reading traditionally appear in

linear order, but the process is circular in nature. We can enjoy the freedom of jumping from one step to another and back again at our own pace as inspired by the Holy Spirit. As a monk said, these are not successive steps but strands of the same cord.

Worry Not

Our relationship with God forms our foundation for sacred reading. As we approach him with trust, believing that he will work and meet us through his Word, we don't have to have an agenda. We have nothing to prove, nor do we need to seek a predetermined outcome from our time of prayer.

Lectio divina should be a tool we use in our walk with God, not a straightjacket that constrains us. Don't let the process of the four steps get in the way of encountering God. On any given day, you might only do one of the steps, or you might do them all. Don't get hung up on the mechanics and forget the purpose—meeting with God and hearing from him through his Word.

Another caution is not to worry too much about any distractions that come along or the random thoughts that pop into your head. They could indicate things on your heart that you can give to God, in which case, you can pray through them. If not, just gently return your attention to the text when you can. You might find it helpful to have a place to write down any details you need to remember or people you want to pray for as they come to mind so that you can release them and return to the practice of sacred reading.

The time given to "meditation" might give us concern. Theologian and Christian martyr Dietrich Bonhoeffer explained why we needn't worry:

> The Word of Scripture should never stop sounding
> in your ears and working in you all day long, just
> like the words of someone you love. And just as you
> do not analyze the words of someone you love, but
> accept them as they are said to you, accept the Word
> of Scripture and ponder it in your heart, as Mary
> did. That is all. That is meditation. . . . [Ask of the
> text,] "What does it say to me?" Then ponder this
> Word long in your heart until it has gone right into
> you and taken possession of you.[5]

As I mentioned earlier, during our time of prayer, we might wonder if anything is happening, while at other times, we might feel deeply moved. In either case, we can develop patience. On the one hand, we shouldn't expect an experience of God each time we read the Bible in this way; on the other hand, when any experiences do happen, we need to weigh them with wisdom and discernment.

If we have only one phrase that strikes us, that's fine! After all, if we were to receive many wonders of God continually, we might start seeking these gifts over the Giver. We might believe that we haven't heard God if he doesn't come to us in this way. Although it can feel painful at times, we learn through silence as well.

Putting It into Practice

Let's explore the four steps of *lectio divina* so that you can experience them yourself. See the suggestions that follow the fourfold description of this practice for which biblical text to choose.

1. *Reading.* As you begin the prayer exercise, quiet yourself before God. You might wish to consider what Bernard of Clairvaux said: "Read in your heart. Become aware of your need of God, whose love never ceases to meet your need, to answer your expectations."[6]

As you consider God's love for you, start reading with silence and awe the section of Scripture you've chosen. Read slowly, being careful to wait for any word the Lord might send you. This slow reading is the so-called honey of God's Word dripping into your mouth.

2. *Reflecting.* Having read the passage once, pause and read it a second time in a spirit of meditating. Ruminate on the words as Mary did when Jesus was born; she "treasured up all these things and pondered them in her heart."[7]

In this second step, let the Scripture interact with your thoughts, hopes, memories, and desires. Let God's Word become his word to you. Perhaps see how the particular word that you gravitate toward reveals Christ in your life.

3. *Responding.* Having read through the passage twice, read it again with an attitude of response. You may sense the movement of the Spirit and not be able to help but respond, whether in thanksgiving, praise, petition, repentance, or adoration. Prayer here is a dialogue with God—a loving conversation with the One who has made you. You might pray

using your voice, your body, your heart as you allow God's Word to touch the deepest part of your being. In so doing, you allow God to transform you into your real self.

4. *Resting.* The fourth step, for modern people, might feel the hardest. Here is where you read through the passage while resting in the presence of the loving Father who uses his words to change you. You need not strive but can practice silence as you simply enjoy being with God. You might be tempted to rush off here, especially if you feel you should be doing something else, or if you sense nothing from the Spirit. But the more you practice slowing down and spending time with God without an agenda, the more you become comfortable with this phase of the exercise. You realize that you don't need to do anything but enjoy the time with God.

As you come to the end of your engagement with the text, commit to God what you've experienced and learned, asking him to help you integrate it into your life as you share his love with others.

Prayer Practice: Circle through the Prayer

You might wonder where to start with sacred reading. The beauty of praying with *lectio divina* is that you can use it with any passage of Scripture—nothing is off limits. For instance, you could start by focusing on a particular book of the Bible and working through it, or you could use the practice with a psalm each day. I like to follow Dallas Willard's recommendation of spending as much time in the Gospels as possible to increase my love for and obedience to Jesus.[8]

Using the fourfold outline, select one of these suggested passages or another of your choosing:

- Psalm 86:11-13: "Teach me your way, LORD . . . ; give me an undivided heart."
- Isaiah 40:28-31: "He gives strength to the weary and increases the power of the weak."
- John 1:1-14: "In the beginning was the Word, and the Word was with God, and the Word was God."
- Ephesians 3:14-21: "I pray that out of his glorious riches he may strengthen you with power through his Spirit in your inner being."
- Revelation 22:1-5: "Then the angel showed me the river of the water of life, as clear as crystal, flowing from the throne of God."

Remember the four steps, knowing that you can move between them:

Reading: Read through the passage the first time, staying open for a word to resonate with you.

Reflecting: Read the passage a second time in a spirit of pondering and meditating, focusing on the word you sensed in the first step.

Responding: Read the passage a third time as you respond to God by giving thanks, interceding, praising, or repenting; then wait to hear from God.

Resting: Read the passage a fourth time in a spirit of
resting; you don't need to do anything—just enjoy
God's presence.

A Worked Example—Praying through a Psalm

If this way of praying is new to you, you might appreciate an
example of how to put it into practice, which is why I share
here how I engaged with Psalm 42:5-8. Note that I followed
the four steps loosely; they are tools to help us meet with
God, not to constrict us.

Why, my soul, are you downcast?
    Why so disturbed within me?
Put your hope in God,
        for I will yet praise him,
        my Savior and my God.
My soul is downcast within me;
        therefore I will remember you
from the land of the Jordan,
        the heights of Hermon—from Mount Mizar.
Deep calls to deep
        in the roar of your waterfalls;
all your waves and breakers
        have swept over me.
By day the LORD directs his love,
        at night his song is with me—
        a prayer to the God of my life.

I read through the passage the first time and pray:

Lord, I ask you to highlight a word or phrase in my mind and heart as I read. Speak to me through your Word. Open me to receive your loving direction and affirmation. I long to hear you, Lord. Thank you for giving us the Bible and these words of the psalmist; speak through them to me.

As I read through the passage, the word *downcast* pops out at me.

Why is my soul downcast, Lord? Why am I looking down at the cares of this world when I should be lifting my head up to you and out to other people?
Why am I so disturbed? Well, I'm worried about our kids—the bullying, the sickness. Questions concerning them weigh me down. Will they thrive in this life? More importantly, will they love and serve you? Lord, I know I need to entrust them to you, for you love them more than I ever will. You know them; you've created them. I *will* put my hope in you; I will praise you, for you are my Savior and my God.

I read the passage a second time, ruminating on the passage. I echo the psalmist who looks back, remembering God from the land of the Jordan, from the heights of the mountain.

Lord, you were there with the psalmist in the good
times and in the hard ones. You were there when
he rejoiced and felt on top of the world. You were
with him in the valley as well, when he felt low and
betrayed. You were there when he couldn't sense your
presence at all.

I know you are with me; you promise never to
leave me. And so why am I looking down, with a
downcast countenance, when you promise never to
abandon me? Why is my soul so disturbed within
me? I will praise you; I will remember you. You call
to me from the deep, sweeping over me with your
love. I put my hope in you.

I turn to the passage a third time and ask God to help me
to respond to his movement in my heart and mind:

I praise you that you can turn my focus away from
myself to you. That you can lift my spirits and help
me to praise again. I lift my chin as an act of obedience,
knowing that you don't want me to wallow. That with
you I affirm your love for my family. I praise you
because I and my family are fearfully and wonderfully
made. You direct your love, and your song is with me.
You are the God of my life, and I worship you.

I read through the passage a final time, asking God to
help me to rest. To help me not to strive for more words or

insights, but to know that he is enough, and I can sit in his presence and be still. He is with me and loves me. I quiet myself further and rest in his love.

Group Prayer Practice:
Leading a Group in Sacred Reading

Experiencing *lectio divina* with others can feel intimidating and strange, and perhaps might even seem incompatible with a group experience. I don't think, for instance, that modern people would find it easy to be among a community of mumblers, such as in a monastery! But doing *lectio divina* in a group can be powerful and meaningful, binding people together.

Feel free to use the following as a guide for facilitating *lectio divina* in a gathering, or you could adapt this for your own prayers.[9] The leader, when introducing the prayer exercise, might want to explain that people could find themselves feeling a bit constrained in this group setting, since they might be asked to move on to the next step before they want to. But they should feel able to stay in whichever step they are in for as long as they wish, trusting that God will meet them in his Word according to their needs.

A benefit of the group approach is sharing experiences after the prayer exercise. One of my favorite parts of leading prayer activities is when people give their accounts of how they encountered God. In my early days of facilitating, I would fret that people wouldn't share, but I've found that after one person has the time to reflect and the courage to speak, many more will follow. The leader should embrace the gift of silence while waiting for that first response.

As you begin the exercise of sacred reading with your chosen passage of Scripture, the leader sets the mood by encouraging people to get into a comfortable, rested posture, setting aside devices and other distractions and turning to the passage. You can close your eyes if you wish.

The leader opens in prayer: Loving Creator, you formed us for communion with you. Lord Jesus Christ, you are the living Word. Comforting Spirit, you bring the Word alive. We ask that you speak to us now through this passage, that we will know your love, grace, and peace. Open our hearts and our minds to hear you.

The leader reads through the passage for the first time, emphasizing that the focus is on reading. Be receptive to the Spirit highlighting a specific word or phrase as the text is read; if one pops out to you, stay with it in the silence.

After a good time of silence (I often set a timer on my phone for three to four minutes in order not to jump ahead), the leader moves the group on to the second stage of sacred reading, that of reflecting. Be open to any thoughts, feelings, or other responses you have to the word that you gravitated toward. Muse and mull over what comes up in God's presence and let your reflections crystallize into key insights that you feel God has for you.

After another period of silence, the leader moves to the third stage, response. Be open to the prayers that arise in you in response to the reading and the word that stood out to you. Are they prayers of petition? Adoration? Intercession? Express them to God in the silence. Respond through a quiet affirmation or through writing down your thoughts and prayers.

After more silence, the leader introduces the fourth stage, rest. Listen to the passage for the fourth time, allowing your whole self to rest in the presence of the Living Word. No more doing; just being. Give yourself over to a quiet surrender.

After a time of silence, the leader closes with a prayer: Father, Son, and Holy Spirit, we thank you that you speak to us through your Word. Confirm to us what you wish for us to take away from this time of prayer. Seal in the work of your Holy Spirit and let nothing that is evil trouble us. Help us to love and serve you more and more.

Then the leader asks for individuals to share with the group, including which word stood out to them, how God through his Spirit interacted with them, and what they learned.

I hope that this practice of sacred reading will become a treasured way of praying through the Bible for you. Taking the time to chew on God's Word, letting it speak to us, can be life-changing. We do so with the help of the indwelling presence of God's Son and Spirit, which we'll turn to next.

3

THE INDWELLING GOD

How to Practice the Presence of God

I SIT IN THE WAITING ROOM, hand on my heart, saying in my mind, *Lord Jesus, you live within me. Come, Holy Spirit, and calm me. Give me your peace. Thank you, Jesus, that you're with me.*

I shift in my seat, trying to still myself as I wait to take my driving test. I'm in my thirties and have been driving for decades but have only recently ventured behind the wheel on the "wrong" side of the road. The English country lanes are narrow, and our car feels big and unwieldy. As I wait, unsure that I will pass this test, I practice the presence of Jesus— I affirm that he is with me. When the driving examiner calls my name, I still feel nervous but also calmer. And although during the test I make eleven minor faults, I pass. Back in the waiting room, I glimpse my husband bearing flowers as I share the good news. He says he figured I'd need them either to celebrate or commiserate.

Practicing the presence of God, as I did while fretting about my driving test, can be done anywhere and at any time. It's simply calling to mind that God dwells within us through his Spirit and his Son. As we consider this wonderful truth, let's stretch ourselves to think about the amazing omnipresent God.

A God Nearby

God, the Creator of the universe, is everywhere. It's mind-blowing to ponder—God's center is everywhere, while God's circumference is nowhere, as philosophers and poets have said.[1] This means that "no atomic particle is so small that God is not fully present to it, and no galaxy is so vast that God does not surround it."[2]

We see this truth in the Bible. As King Solomon brought the Ark of the Lord's Covenant to the new Temple he built to honor God, the Lord's presence filled the Temple as a cloud.[3] Solomon then dedicated this ornate building to God while he wondered at the mystery of God coming to earth: "Will God really dwell on earth? The heavens, even the highest heaven, cannot contain you. How much less this temple I have built!"[4] And the Lord responded yes, he was there in the Temple; his Name would be there forever: "My eyes and my heart will always be there."[5] God promises never to leave his people.

The prophets underlined the same truth. For instance, Isaiah said that God lives in a "high and holy place" but also with those who are lowly and humble.[6] Jeremiah, in turn, acted as the mouthpiece for God, who thundered out this truth:

Am I only a God nearby . . .
     and not a God far away?
Who can hide in secret places
     so that I cannot see them? . . .
Do not I fill heaven and earth?[7]

Time and time again God seeks to reassure—or convict—his people that he lives on the earth.

Then God became a man in the form of his Son, Jesus. In the last words of the Gospel of Matthew, he told his disciples: "Surely I am with you always, to the very end of the age."[8] From the beginning of God's Word, when he was in the Garden of Eden with our first parents, to John's Revelation, where God promises to welcome his people into the Eternal City, he assures us of his never-ending presence with us.

If God is everywhere, are we aware of him? Or do we take this truth for granted? When we practice being mindful and aware of him, we open ourselves to the wonder of him and his creation. We can experience his presence when we're living in the present moment, right here, right now. Instead of being preoccupied with things that might not even happen, we affirm that God is with us.

In doing so we can ask God to help us focus on one thing at a time. For instance, we can enjoy a moment of truly seeing something, whether another person, a flower, a pine cone, a leaf. After all, if we can't revel in God's creation, how can we hope to experience the unseen God?

Prayer Practice: God with Us
Becoming aware of God in our daily lives takes being intentional. Why not try this today or tomorrow?

You wake, and as you stretch, you place your hand on your heart and affirm, "Jesus lives within me." As you pour your beverage of choice, thank God for the gift of this new day, for life and food and drink and most of all that he is with you.

When it's time to get cleaned up, as you feel the water in the bath or shower, ponder the gift of living water, Jesus who washes us clean and forgives our sins. He slakes our thirst and refreshes us. Thank him again for his presence with you and ask him to remind you, each time you wash your hands today, that he is with you.

While getting dressed, think of Jesus removing your rags, those stained and dirty clothes you feel ashamed of. No longer are you defined by your sins and wrongdoing, for *he* clothes you. His presence within you changes you from the inside out. Now you're wearing the robes of a beloved child, an heir of the King.

Perhaps in the next part of your day, you leave home to travel to what awaits you. You might be tempted to think of the journey as empty time, a necessary part of getting from one place to another. Today, remember that Jesus goes with you. If you encounter delays and annoyances that make your heart beat faster, ask him to give you his peace and patience.

You come to one of your main activities of the day, whether working on a project for your job or school, attending a social engagement, caring for a child, volunteering at a local organization, or something else. Welcome Jesus into whatever you are doing. Remember that he'll never leave you, that he will bring you comfort, encouragement, conviction, peace, and joy. You might want to set a timer at various intervals to remind yourself to call to mind the presence of Jesus.

Sometime during your day, if you're able, take a break to go for a walk with Jesus. In your imagination, clasp his hand as you stroll along, either chatting through your day or just enjoying the silence together. As you walk, take in the beauty of your surroundings, especially if you're in nature, or ponder the wonder of human ingenuity in the buildings around you. Listen for birdsong as you take a deep breath, reveling in the amazing truth that the God of the universe would dwell within you through his Son and his Spirit.

As you spend time with others, really notice them. Consider that they, too, are made in the image of God, and if they follow Jesus, he lives within them also. Moment by moment he is changing them more into his likeness. If you are in conflict with someone, ask God to reveal to you who that person really is. Ask the Holy Spirit to lead you to a good resolution of your issues, if possible, and to show you where you're at fault, if you are.

It's time for your main meal. Maybe you're eating with family or friends; perhaps you're on your own. If you're alone, remember that Christ is with you. Either way, you can set a place at your table to signify his presence with you. As you eat, think about or discuss how much Jesus enjoyed his meals with others. And how he said that he is the Bread of Life, and that when we believe in him, we won't hunger. He feeds us with his food, which truly satisfies.

As you come to the end of your day with Jesus, think back over it, from morning to night. Bring to mind the moments when you remembered that Jesus was with you, and those when you didn't. Perhaps you experienced a deep sense of peace, a feeling of well-being in your spirit and your body, that God gave to you as you practiced his presence. You might want to write down how you sensed God's presence and what that means to you.

Ask God through his Holy Spirit to give you sweet sleep, with no nightmares to darken your dreams, that you'll wake refreshed.

The Indwelling God

We've seen how God is always here among us—always with us. Another wonderful mystery is that he dwells within us through his Son and his Spirit.

In the Old Testament, God filled only certain people with his presence, usually his prophets, who spoke on his behalf.

Moses acknowledged this when he told Joshua off for being jealous about the Lord filling seventy of the elders in the camp with his Spirit. Moses said to Joshua, "Are you jealous for my sake? I wish that all the LORD's people were prophets and that the LORD would put his Spirit on them!"[9] Another instance is when God called Ezekiel to his role as a prophet. The Lord said, "I will put my Spirit in you and move you to follow my decrees and be careful to keep my laws."[10] The New Testament brims with examples of how God lives in his people. I love exploring this theme in John's Gospel and through the letters of the apostle Paul.[11]

Prayer Practice: The Vine and the Branches

Let's pray through what's known as Jesus' Last Discourse and engage with the images of Jesus as the Vine and us as the branches.[12]

Ponder the story. In John 14:31, Jesus says, "Come now; let us leave." He and his friends have just enjoyed their last supper together, and Judas has gone off to betray him. As Jesus and his disciples walk toward the garden of Gethsemane, they pass the symbol of a vine over the Temple, which signified God's people in the Old Testament. Jesus shares what will happen after he dies, how he is the Vine and his Father is the gardener who prunes the branches (his followers). This amazing image of Jesus being the Vine, giving life to us as the branches who are connected to him, reveals the reality of union with God through Christ. We find this union by following Jesus' instructions: "Remain in me, as I also remain in you."[13] Through being united to him, with the sap of the Holy Spirit transporting the nourishment from the Vine to the branches, we bear fruit.

Picture a grapevine and its branches, the wood of the vine gnarled and rough with branches springing out of it. Consider how the vine needs the branches, and the branches need the vine: without branches, the vine won't produce fruit, and without the vine, the branches won't receive the necessary nutrients to live. This image points to one of the amazing truths of the Christian faith: that God through Christ condescends to make his home in us. That is, although he is all-powerful and all-knowing, he restricts himself to working in and through us with all of our limitations and failings.[14] Spend some time engaging with this truth in a way that feels best to you. You might want to draw a vine and branches, sketching the contours of the trunk and the new growth and dead wood attached to it. Maybe you'd like to go for a walk in nature, taking time to gaze at trees and their branches. Or perhaps you'd like to write a poem, sing a song, or talk with a friend or family member, sharing your feelings about branches and trees and union with God.

After Jesus speaks of the vine, he prays for his disciples and the disciples to come—us! I love how succinctly Jesus states this mind-and-heart-stretching truth in his prayer: May they "be one, Father, just as you are in me and I am in you" and "that they may be one as we are one—I in them and you in me—so that they may be brought to complete unity."[15] Chew on how Jesus is in the Father, we are in Jesus, and he is in us. He dwells in us not just for our own edification, but that we would be united with others.

Spend some time praying through Jesus' prayer for the disciples who were with him and his prayer for the disciples to come,[16] knowing that even when Jesus was alive, he prayed specifically for you. Put his prayer into your own words so it sinks deeply into your inner being. Ask God to reveal something about how he dwells in you through the Son and the Holy Spirit.

Know that as you practice the presence of Jesus, you're affirming the truth of your union with him. Remind yourself today that Christ lives within you as you go about your activities, and seek not to forget. Just as a fish is made mostly of water and lives in the water, so are we surrounded by God—he's around us and in us. And just as a fish is blind to the water it lives in, so can we overlook God's presence.[17] Through the practice of affirming his presence within, we remember.

Practicing the Presence

We may best recognize the phrase "practicing the presence of God" from Brother Lawrence, a lay monk who lived in the 1600s in France. Although he wanted to enter a religious order as a monk, he couldn't read or write, so he was sent to work in the monastery kitchen. Frustrated by the clamor and noise around him and stymied in his desire to spend his time in prayer, he was also hampered by a war injury and called himself clumsy. Yet he resigned himself to his kitchen work.

But eventually Brother Lawrence started to commit himself fully to God, seeking to spend each moment in God's presence while in the kitchen—even with several people talking at once and all of the mess and activity that's needed to feed a group of people. God changed him over the years as he recalled that God was with him, right there among the pots and pans. The peace and joy he experienced, even in the midst of his physical pain and limitations, shone from within him. People noticed his infectious contentment, and monks and others would visit him to seek his advice. Through his letters to these visitors, collected after his death, we have the treasures of this humble lay brother.

His phrase "practice the presence" simply means calling to mind that Christ dwells within us. We remind ourselves of his presence, focusing our attention on God as we welcome him into the middle of our lives. As Brother Lawrence said, "My prayers are nothing other than a sense of the presence of God."[18]

An example I love is how he had to travel to buy some wine for his monastery. Because of his lack of business sense and his proneness to trip and fall, he found it an unwelcome task. But he "told the Lord that it was His business" that he was about, and therefore he had no uneasiness as he fulfilled the task. Everything went well—no spills or mishaps.[19]

His secret to peace and well-being was holding a continual conversation with God throughout the day—a "free and simple" discussion with him: "We need to recognize that God is always intimately present with us and address Him every moment."[20] I like how one of my friends in her distinct Yorkshire accent puts it: "My way of praying is wittering with God throughout the day." She keeps a running conversation with God in the retreat center she and her husband run, and like Brother Lawrence, she combines her internal conversation with the daily communal prayers.

Practicing the presence of Jesus won't happen unless we're intentional about it—it's a life-enhancing habit that we build into our lives. Making this practice a habit takes time, and of course we'll fail to remember now and again, just as we fall short in other areas of life. When we do, Brother Lawrence simply advises us to admit our faults to God, reminding him that if he doesn't help us, we'll keep on failing. We can ask God frankly and plainly for his help to make us more like Jesus in our thoughts, words, and actions.

Again, we might not feel anything specific when we're practicing the presence of God. I wonder if he sometimes removes a tangible sense of his presence from us when we become too dependent on our feelings and think he's only with us when we have an emotional response. He teaches us to use our will, not to depend on our emotions. After all, it's called *practicing* the presence for a reason—we keep on keeping on with it.

Practicing the presence of Jesus is a great antidote not only when we overemphasize our emotions but also when we need to take the attention off ourselves and look to God. Through this exercise, we can stop listening to any negative voices that fill our minds as we instead receive God's love and affirmation. As we do so, he'll bring us what we need, whether a word of love, knowledge that he leads and guides us, the healing balm for our hurts, or perhaps a sudden inspiration and answer to the dilemma before us. As we sit in his presence, God showers us with his wisdom and love like flakes of gold swirling down from the skies.

Prayer Practice:
Follow Brother Lawrence's Instructions
Brother Lawrence's gentle but insistent directions appear throughout his letters. Read his instructions through several times today or tomorrow, perhaps after you eat your meals, and then put them into action. If you're inclined, you could take a photo of this list so it's with you on your phone.[21]

> Begin!
> Be daring.
> Lift your heart to God.
> Ask for his grace.
> Don't get weighed down by a lot of rules.
> Recall God to mind as often as possible.
> Have a secret conversation with him.
> Set your mind on God.
> Make it your business to be in the Lord's presence.
> Resolve to never again willfully stray from God.
> Hold yourself before God.
> Think often of God, by day and by night.
> Turn your mind to the presence of Christ.

Fix your mind on Jesus.

The Lord dwells within you—seek him there!

Return to God.

Do everything for the love of God.

Agree that you'll live with the Lord all your days.

Know that you're helpless without God.

Worship God as often as you can.

Apply yourself to seeking and obeying God with diligence.

Keep your mind in his holy presence.

Continually talk with God.

Confess to God, "I cannot do this unless you help me."

Speak to God frankly and plainly.

Ask God for his help throughout your day.

Prayer Practice: Practicing the Presence of God

Affirm God's presence within throughout the day. Here are some more suggestions for how to do so:

- Memorize key passages of the Bible to ponder in the morning, afternoon, and evening.
- Set an alarm on your phone at various intervals to stop and pray.
- Commit to practicing the presence every time you engage in a repeated activity, such as washing your hands or getting yourself something to drink.
- Place your hand on your heart to affirm that Christ lives within you.

Praying without Ceasing

Brother Lawrence is the best-known monastery dweller who introduced the concept of practicing the presence of God. But a monk from an earlier time was also keen about praying without ceasing. John Cassian, born around 365 in what's now Romania, has been called a founder of the Western mystical tradition. Wanting to help the uneducated monks in his care become increasingly devoted to Christ, he created a formula for prayer. In this he followed Paul's admonition to the Thessalonians to "pray continually."[22] For the basis of the prayer, Cassian looked to Psalm 70:1, stating in a sermon, "To keep the thought of God always in your mind you must cling totally to this formula for piety: 'Come to my help, O God; Lord, hurry to my rescue.'"[23]

Why did he choose this particular verse out of all of Scripture? He had several reasons:

- It carries with it all of the feelings that people are capable of.
- It can be adapted to every condition in life.
- It is a cry to God for help in the face of danger.
- It is a means of expressing humility and our limitations.
- It brings with it the assurance of being heard and that help is always present.[24]

In short, this verse reveals God to those who call to him, for he is never far away from those he loves.

Cassian's instructions as to when we can and should pray this psalm seem up-to-date, such as when a passion for eating assails us, or when a headache keeps us from reading, or when sleep eludes us. We might echo Cassian's remarks: "I see myself worn down by sleeplessness over many nights and shut away from all the refreshment of my night's rest. And so I must sigh and pray, 'Come to my help, O God; Lord, hurry to my rescue.'"[25]

Praying with a short burst from the Psalms can be lifegiving when, for example, our patience is tested by standing in a long line or when we're in the midst of a conflict with someone. Asking God for help and assurance can center our hearts and minds, reminding us of God's love and promise that he will work in our lives.

But this prayer practice shouldn't feel like a straitjacket; after all, even Cassian admitted that he couldn't pray only this verse from the Psalms, for he craved variety and found his formula monotonous. However, although his prayer method has limitations, we can incorporate it into our lives as one of many ways to pray.[26]

Prayer Practice: Pray with Cassian

Cassian's prayer can be applied to various situations. Take a moment to read through each of the following scenarios prayerfully and ask God to be with you.

- Fighting against sin: *Come to my help, O God; Lord, hurry to my rescue!*

- Struggling with dried-up desire: *Come to my help,
  O God; Lord, hurry to my rescue!*
- Fighting rage, greed, or gloom: *Come to my help,
  O God; Lord, hurry to my rescue!*
- Being tempted by boredom: *Come to my help, O God;
  Lord, hurry to my rescue!*
- Sensing that demons surround you: *Come to my help,
  O God; Lord, hurry to my rescue!*
- Feeling close to God: *Come to my help, O God; Lord,
  hurry to my rescue!*

Prayer Practice: Breath Prayers

Cassian used the verse from Psalm 70 as a way to express his needs and desires at any given moment. A similar prayer practice relies on something even more elemental to us than the Psalms—our breath. Along these lines, I sent a friend some "breath prayers." As a mother in Britain, she's concerned about which secondary school her son will be going to, for children here attend these schools from the age of eleven up to sixteen or eighteen, and thus the school forms a key part of their education. Having heard that her son wasn't allocated the school they had hoped for, she's now playing the unwanted waiting game of seeing which school has a place for him in September, six months away. Instead of fretting, I hope she can pray. (Which is what I say to myself in uncertain times as well!)

Breath praying can be a simple but profound exercise. As you inhale, pray one word, and then as you exhale, pray the other. Or pray one syllable of a word as you draw a breath, and then pray the second syllable as you let it go:

Fa-ther
Je-sus
Spir-it

You can also focus on asking God through his Spirit to take something from you and fill you with his attributes:

Lord, I give you my anxiety,
I receive your peace.

I release my fear,
I welcome your love.

I hand over my fretting,
I accept your guidance.

I exhale my stress,
I inhale your rest.

You can pray special lines from Scripture this way too:

The LORD is my shepherd;
I shall not want.

PSALM 23:1, KJV

Speak, LORD,
for your servant is listening.

1 SAMUEL 3:9

[You love me] with an everlasting love.
    [You draw me] with unfailing kindness.

JEREMIAH 31:3

The LORD . . . is with [me],
    the Mighty Warrior who saves.

ZEPHANIAH 3:17

Keep me as the apple of your eye;
    hide me in the shadow of your wings.

PSALM 17:8

In you
    my soul takes refuge.

PSALM 57:1, ESV

Taste and see
    that the LORD is good.

PSALM 34:8

You are
    my hiding place.

PSALM 32:7

He tends his flock
    like a shepherd.

ISAIAH 40:11

When I can't sleep, I often pray these words attributed to English poet Thomas Traherne (c. 1636–1674):

Lord, have mercy
Into Thy hands
Thee I adore

Group Prayer Practice: Christ's Presence in Our Present

When I lead church groups or retreats, I often set aside time for us to practice the presence of God together. There's something special about doing so as a group, not only sharing the experience itself, but also hearing how God meets us in our time together. I've often led the following exercise to help us focus on the present moment and God's presence within it.

1. Opening with prayer. *The leader calls participants to quiet themselves and get into a comfortable but alert position, perhaps closing their eyes. Then the leader begins with an opening prayer:* "Lord Jesus, you bring us to the Father through the help of the Holy Spirit. Thank you that you are with us even here, even now. Open our hearts and our minds to receive you. Still us and

help us turn from anything that may distract us, that we will be fully present here with you."

2. Adopting a receptive posture. *The leader guides the time of reflection, encouraging participants to rest their hands on their laps with their palms facing up as a symbol of being open and receptive to the work of the Holy Spirit.* The leader continues, "Know that Christ Jesus is Lord over all that has been, all that is, and all that is to come. But we meet him in the here and now, in the present moment. We bring our whole selves to God now."

3. Opening to God in prayer. *The leader tells the group to clench both of their hands into fists and then guides them through the exercise:* "While holding your fists tightly, become aware of all the things from past moments and past days that occupy your thoughts and feelings right now. Imagine that you are holding them all tightly in your left hand. Think about a closed hand and how it signifies that you're not allowing any space for Christ to come into it. So in your own time, relax your left hand and turn your palm upward as you release these thoughts, feelings, and events into Christ's care.

"Now become aware of all that's ahead of you—the concerns, feelings, worries, things to do, and even the things you're looking forward to. Imagine that you're clenching them in your right hand. Your fist begins to tire, the presence of tension wearing it down. When you're ready, open your hand as a symbol of letting go of these concerns and worries into Christ's care as you trust him with the outcome.

"With both of your hands open, palms upward, express to God a willingness to respond and receive from Christ whatever he wants to fill you with in the here and now. Stay for a moment in the quiet, consciously enjoying God's presence in the present as you offer this time, this place, yourself to him to use as he chooses.

"Know that Christ Jesus is Lord over all that has been, all that is, and all that is to come. And he is with us now. Thanks be to God."

4. Holding silence and sharing. *The leader ends with a period of silence and then asks members of the group if they would like to share what they experienced during the exercise.*[27]

Prayer Practice: Embracing Silence

Sometimes silence can feel painful and strained, yet other moments overflow with peace and contentment. Let's spend some time with God in silence as we contemplate him, asking him to fill us with his presence. Some of the following prayers are inspired by the classic medieval work *The Cloud of Unknowing.*[28]

Sit comfortably but stay alert. Start with a prayer: "Lord God, fill me with your presence and be present in these moments together. Keep away anything that is not of you. Quell any distractions that pop into my mind and help me put them to one side. I welcome you and thank you for being here with me."

You may wish to place your hands on your knees, palms facing up, as a physical reminder of your openness to God's presence. As you quiet your heart and mind, rest in the knowledge that God is with you. Relax—he isn't going anywhere. Trust that he is with you.

Lift your heart to God, seeking him with love. As much as you can, forget the world and all that is within it, letting go. If your mind starts to wander, gently bring it back to God. To help refocus your thoughts, you might want to slowly say the words "Father. Jesus. Spirit."

As you release any thoughts that distract you, turn back to God and seek to be united with him through Christ. Don't struggle or strive; work at being present to him until the longing to know him springs up from within you. Be careful not to enter into contemplation of him as merely an intellectual exercise. It won't come that way; it comes through your mind *and* your heart.

At first in the silence, you might sense only darkness— a cloud of unknowing, as it were. You might feel it's incomprehensible, but still you keep on reaching for God. Be resolved to wait in this lack of knowing as long as necessary, and don't give up. Continue longing to know the God whom you love. Through God's mercy, you will achieve your heart's desire to see him and feel him in this life.

You may have some moments where the clouds open, even a crack. You may sense the weight of God's presence. Or you may not. Don't strive, and don't despair if you feel nothing. Trust that God is with you. Wait in the silence and know that he is there. With time and practice, you'll discern his voice or his presence.

When you feel ready to move on from your time of contemplation, you may wish to pray with the author of *The Cloud of Unknowing*: "God, to whom all hearts are open, to whom all wills speak and from whom no secret is hid, I beg you so to cleanse the intent of my heart with the unutterable gift of your grace that I may perfectly love you and worthily praise you. Amen."[29]

We've seen how God fills us with his loving, affirming presence through his Son and Spirit. We're never alone; he's always with us. Knowing this amazing truth gives us the courage when we pray to listen for his response, which is what we'll explore next.

4

HEARING GOD

How to Listen in Prayer

GIVE UP YOUR CAMPAIGN.

After these words pop into my head, I slam my journal closed. In search of a distraction, I pick up a book, but the words blur on the page. I'm in a spacious room at a retreat center in the south of England for a long-anticipated time away with God. To hear God's gentle but insistent statement right at the start sends me into an emotional mess. The campaign in question is my desire to move to the States, where our kids could grow up knowing the land of my birth, we'd be closer to my American family, and I wouldn't feel like an outsider. But God asks me to give up this campaign? I can't countenance the thought. I spend the rest of the retreat reading, sleeping, taking walks, and generally avoiding God and his big directive.

For me this example of hearing God stands out because the four words seemed to come so clearly from outside of me. I didn't hear them audibly; instead, they appeared in my mind. The words had a depth and insistence that made me take them seriously, which as I tested them out led me to believe that they were from God.

Over the years of my adventures of listening to God, I've learned to obey him when I discern that what I'm hearing is from him. So in the weeks and months after that retreat, I started to relinquish my desires and demands to move across the Atlantic. I purposely stopped talking about an impending move with my American family; I bought bookcases; I accepted as a gift an expensive kitchen appliance that wouldn't work in the States because of the different voltage.

Letting my dream die filled me with longing and pain. But what I didn't realize in my confusion and loss was how I would grow in contentment and joy while not trying to live in two countries simultaneously. God's gentle urging while I was on that retreat was not only for my good but for the good of my family as well.

"Here I Am"
Our Bibles burst with God speaking to his children, from Genesis when he walked in the Garden with our first parents, Adam and Eve, to Revelation and the vision he gave

the aging disciple John. One well-loved example of God's communication is the account of young Samuel when he was living in the Temple and serving the nearly blind Eli.[1] Set apart for God by his mother, Hannah, Samuel slept in the Temple near the Ark of the Covenant, probably in semi-permanent rooms. As he slumbered he heard a summons and immediately thought it was Eli. He reacted in the manner of a servant, the same humble response of Moses and Abraham before him: "Here I am."

But Eli didn't call him; the older priest sent him back to bed. After this happened two more times, Eli realized that God was calling Samuel, so Eli instructed him how to respond. Samuel obeyed and presented himself to God: "Speak, LORD, for your servant is listening."[2] God spoke, giving him a message of judgment for Eli because he hadn't stamped out the sins of his sons.

Note that Samuel needed help from someone more experienced to hear God, and even his older mentor took some time to figure out that God was speaking. This first calling of Samuel marked the beginning of his role as a prophet. He became a reliable messenger who spoke the word of the Lord, with none of his words falling to the ground.[3]

The Sheep Hear the Shepherd

In the New Testament, we have none other than God himself speaking in human form. In John's Gospel, Jesus told the Pharisees a powerful parable that revealed how God speaks to his children and how we can respond:

The gatekeeper opens the gate for [the shepherd], and the sheep listen to his voice. He calls his own sheep by name and leads them out. When he has brought out all his own, he goes on ahead of them, and his sheep follow him because they know his voice. But they will never follow a stranger; in fact, they will run away from him because they do not recognize a stranger's voice.[4]

When Jesus calls himself the Good Shepherd and says that we are his sheep, he hearkens back to Old Testament imagery. For instance, in Ezekiel God said, "As a shepherd looks after his scattered flock when he is with them, so will I look after my sheep."[5] And this theme, of course, appears in the beloved Psalm 23.

Some background on Middle Eastern sheep and shepherds can help us understand Jesus' words better. Back then, sheep pens would hold several herds in their large walled enclosures that backed up to a cliff or canyon. The gatekeeper—the hired hand—would guard the sole gate so that wild animals couldn't attack the sheep.

In the morning the various shepherds would come to collect their herds. The sheep would recognize the voice of their shepherd, following him alone. These shepherds, devoted to their sheep, talked and sang to them or played a flute. They'd often name each sheep in the flock, usually after a specific physical characteristic. And Middle Eastern shepherds wouldn't drive their sheep from the back but would lead them from the front.

From this parable we learn that we as sheep are vulnerable creatures who Jesus says are precious to him, whom he knows by name. He doesn't barrel us forward in ways we don't want to go but rather leads us from the front, gently calling us and beckoning us forward.

His leadership is sacrificial and intimate: "I am the good shepherd; I know my sheep and my sheep know me—just as the Father knows me and I know the Father—and I lay down my life for the sheep."[6] Jesus emphasizes the deep knowing between him and his sheep. In fact, our relationship with him is modeled on the relationship of deep love and communion between him and his Father.

The stories of Samuel and of Jesus as the Good Shepherd not only deepen our understanding of how God speaks to us but also provide us with rich food for our imaginations.[7]

Prayer Practice:
Opening Our Hearts to the Still, Small Voice

Let's pause to pray, taking some time to listen for God's still, small voice using Scripture as a springboard. You can engage with this prayer exercise according to the way you prefer, such as writing out your prayers and God's response, or speaking out the conversation, or expressing your prayers through some kind of creative act such as sketching or painting. Don't feel overly constrained by my questions; if you feel God leading you in another direction, follow the Spirit.

Our passage is from one of John's letters, which we'll use to converse with God about our identity in him.

> See what great love the Father has lavished on us, that we should be called children of God! And that is what we are! The reason the world does not know us is that it did not know him. Dear friends, now we are children of God, and what we will be has not yet been made known. But we know that when Christ appears, we shall be like him, for we shall see him as he is.[8]

- Open your heart and mind to God through his Spirit, welcoming him to speak to you. Ask that he would calm you and bring you to a place of receptivity that you might hear him. Ask him also to limit anything that may hinder you, whether from within or outside of you, as you express yourself and listen to him.

- Praise God that he is your Father and that you are his child. Ask him to lavish his love on you—you could stand and stretch out your arms or cup your hands in a position of receiving. You might want to chat through what being his child means to you.

- Tell God what you think about the world not knowing us as Christians because they don't know him. Ask him for any insights or wisdom about this truth from John's letter.

- John says that as his child, you don't yet know what you will be. What do you want to be? Ask God to untangle any mixture of emotions you may have about who you are and who you will be and wait for his response.

- Ponder the promise of Christ appearing and that we'll be made like him when we see him face-to-face. What does this mean for you today? Express your thoughts and feelings to God. What does the Spirit bring to mind as you wait for a word, picture, song, or something else?

- As your conversation comes to an end, commit yourself again to God, and ask him to confirm all that is good in what you've heard and help you dismiss anything that is not of him.

Hearing God in Daily Life

As we learn to hear God's voice during our times of prayer, we'll find ourselves becoming more open to his nudges throughout the day. Some time ago I was on the way to the gym, eager not to be late so that I could snag my favorite spot in the front corner. I parked the car and started toward the gym when I realized I had my watch on, which I don't like to wear while I'm working out. As I kept walking, I had the thought that I should go back and put my watch in the car. You guessed it. I ignored that nudge, and sure enough I lost my lovely eco watch that day.

Was the prompt from the Holy Spirit, or was it "just me"? I can't tell you for sure, but I wouldn't be surprised if it was the Spirit. God the Father cares for us as his children; just as earthly parents would tell their kids to put a treasured possession in a safe place, so he could seek to warn one of his beloved.

That ignored nudge, and the need to buy another watch, made me eager to discern and follow the Spirit's prompts in my daily life. Several months later as I was returning from a walk by a nearby brook, I passed by a nail on the ground. I kept on walking but then felt a prompt to go back, pick it up, and throw it away. This time I obeyed the nudge. Was this the Spirit or "just me"? Again, I can't say for sure. But maybe my little action saved a child from harm. Perhaps what's more important is my increased awareness of these inner urges and my willingness to follow them. The more I pay attention to them and train myself to act on them—using my God-given common sense, of course—the more I will notice them. And the more God can use and train me.

Just last week as I was walking down the street in our bit of north London, I paused at the stoplight and then, sensing an urge within, decided to go a different way. I enjoyed the sun on my face and was lost in a bit of a reverie when moments later I heard my name being called. I searched and saw a lovely familiar face—a friend for whom I'd been praying, who was moving in just two days' time. As I waved goodbye after a wonderful chat, I breathed, *Thank you, Lord. Thank you for her and thank you for those little nudges in my spirit by your Spirit. Keep on speaking.*

As a prayer exercise, why not commit to opening yourself

up to God's Spirit throughout the day (or tomorrow if you're reading this at night)? Then review your day with God before you go to sleep, asking him to remind you of the ways he communicated with you. Notice what you were doing when you sensed his voice, how you felt, how you responded, how you tested out what you heard, and what happened as a result of this communication.

Strapping on Roller Skates

Hearing God is not just an individual activity. When a group comes together to listen on behalf of each other, God may move in surprising ways. At a weekend retreat focused on listening prayer, I sat in a circle with four other people I had just met. A lovely German couple had introduced the topic, combining an openness to how the Spirit of God could move in our lives with the need for wisdom and discernment. In our circle, as we embarked on this practice of listening to God on behalf of each other, I grew a bit nervous but was also excited for my turn.

For each person, we would set a timer for seven minutes and then listen to God in a spirit of humility and active openness, jotting down notes and drawing pictures of what floated into our minds. When the buzzer rang, each of us would share our impressions, with a designated scribe taking notes.

When it was my turn for people to listen on my behalf, I took several minutes to settle into the quiet as I tried to stop wondering what others might be hearing. As the Holy Spirit gave me peace, the main image that came was me sitting by a campfire with God breathing on me, for he wanted me to be warm. Since it was January and I was living in a cold and drafty Victorian vicarage, I assumed the picture could have a literal interpretation—at least I hoped it would! And indeed, over the following years, my husband was able to make our home warmer, which helped me not only physically but emotionally and spiritually too.

But what really stood out from the circle of prayer was a picture one of the others had of roller skates. He said that when you first strap on the skates, it feels scary and out of control. But as you push through, you can eventually experience fun. I knew immediately what the picture related to—my public speaking. Not long before, I'd ventured into sharing with church groups and other gatherings but had found the experiences nerve wracking. As I spoke, I would be glued behind the lectern and wed to my fully written-out text. I was scared of falling.

His picture of the roller skates proved apt, as thereafter I sought God's help to feel the wind in my hair. As I strapped on the skates, standing before a group of people, I became more confident, learning to speak from briefer notes and to trust God more freely instead of scripting out the content so tightly. I could gaze out at the people, seeing them with love as I moved away from the perceived safety of the lectern. As I gained some speed on my skates, I felt exhilaration and joy.

This group exercise of listening prayer is something I've facilitated when I lead retreats, and each time I'm grateful and encouraged by how God sparks people's minds and hearts for each other through his Spirit. A main reason that this exercise works so well relates to wisdom and discernment. On the one hand, those who share their thoughts and ideas must resist giving any kind of interpretation or application, and on the other hand, the one who receives the offerings must test them out.

This is the aspect that the wonderful German couple, whose names I failed to note, emphasized so brilliantly.[9] When listening to God on behalf of others in a group, we need to be open to the work of the Spirit, inviting God to move in and through us, but when we receive from God for someone else, we must refrain from guessing what that picture or Scripture or word could mean in that person's life. After all, not only do we not know what's going on in someone's heart and mind, but we might also have heard wrong! And when we conjecture the meaning of the word, images, songs, or Scripture, we rob people of coming to their own understanding through the help of the Holy Spirit.

Interestingly, four of the five offerings from around the circle (including my own) had some value to me, but over the years I forgot them, remembering them only when I returned to my notes from the day. They didn't have the life-changing power of that sole image of the roller skates. That picture resonated with me immediately and deeply—it was a gift from God. The other words and images gave life and help at the time as I held them before God, weighing them, but they didn't have the strong impact of that particular image.

Listening on behalf of others can be a way of birthing God's gifts of grace, peace, hope, and love. Once when I was leading this exercise with a small group in Spain, we experienced this birthing image wonderfully. Throughout the morning as we set the timer for each individual, seeking to hear God's voice for each person with all of our energy and focus, we could hear little yelps through the open window of a mama cat birthing her litter of kittens. We loved the synergy of the physical and spiritual births at the same time.

Prayer Practice: Hearing God with Others

As you prepare to listen to God on behalf of the others in your group, remember that God's Spirit is like the wind, blowing where it wishes.[10] We can't grab it. You might want to picture snowflakes gently falling from the sky. We can't snatch those either, but we can hold open our hands to receive them.

Listening to God for others can be especially meaningful when members of the group don't know one another well. Our desires for those close to us can crowd into our experience of listening and threaten to overshadow God's voice. If you can arrange the groups accordingly, putting people with others they don't know well, do so. If not, be aware of this potential influence, asking God to help everyone rein in those feelings.

The seven minutes of listening for each person is long enough to give you the space and freedom to get quiet before God but not so long that you start to despair that the time will never end. Recognize that you may feel anxious as you wait for God's Spirit—you may hear the person next to you grab her phone to make a note, while the person on the other side opens his Bible, rustling the pages. Yet you sense nothing. You could inhale deeply, reminding yourself that God's Spirit lives in you. You could put your hand on your heart, asking God to calm your nerves. Or you could breathe out short arrow prayers for those next to you, rejoicing that they seem to be hearing from God.

The distractions might be mundane—you realize you need to go to the bathroom, you wonder what's happening at home, you imagine what you'll have for dinner. You can welcome these distractions as guests to the exercise but tell them they need to sit quietly at the side, waiting their turn! If you suddenly remember something urgent that you don't want to forget, simply make a note of it and then return to the exercise of listening.

As you wait in the silence, you may sense a thought coming to the fore—the melody or refrain from a song, an image that pops into your mind, the fragments of a Scripture verse you suddenly remember, a reference for a text from the Bible. Don't lunge at the ideas and images but rest quietly as they come—think again of not grabbing the snowflake but letting it land in your open hand. So, too, let the picture or word settle in your heart, and when you're ready, jot it down.

You may wonder, *Is this really God speaking? Is it just me? Is it the devil?* Seek not to evaluate what you're sensing but instead entrust that to the person for whom you're listening. Know, too, however, that words from the evil one go against the wisdom of the Bible and seek to make you break God's commands. We can discern them perhaps more easily than words rooted in our hearts and desires, which can be more difficult to weigh before God.

Come to the exercise with humility, knowing that you may get it wrong. As we learn from our mistakes, we trust that God can use us even though we *hear* "through a glass, darkly," to bend the metaphor from 1 Corinthians 13:12 (KJV).

Once everyone is settled into their groups, the designated leader gives the opening comments, making sure each person understands the process and the hopes for the time together. The leader assigns one person as the timekeeper and one as a scribe—it can be helpful to move these tasks from person to person.

Before starting the first seven-minute segment, the leader prays for the whole of the experience, asking God to send the Holy Spirit to guide each person and to restrict any movement of the evil one. After asking God for openness and receptivity along with faith and hope, the leader then signals the start of the seven minutes, the timekeeper setting the alarm on their phone.

When the time is up, everyone shares one at a time, with the scribe noting the images and words. Share what you receive without comment or interpretation, holding the images and words lightly. Say, for example, "I saw a picture of a deep well, a pool of calm water with small ripples in it." Don't say, "I saw a pool of deep water, which symbolizes your identity in God. Those waters are filled with his living water. You need to immerse yourself in them daily."

When you're on the receiving end, test out what you hear with God, the Bible, your common sense, circumstances, and, as appropriate, other people you trust. If God is behind the words, you may feel them fly straight into your heart. If they feel off base, let them pass you by and don't overly try to figure out what they might mean. Know also that it might take time for God to make clear what a word or image means.

Learning to Discern

As I mentioned in the introduction of this book, my journey of learning to hear God started in earnest in my twenties when, after a failed relationship, I plummeted into God's arms. In my pain and anguish over life not turning out how I had planned, I started to experience a new depth of intimacy with God. The Bible came alive as I started to sense God's still, small voice speaking lovingly to me.

Hearing God's words of loving affirmation opened up a deep space of receiving within, and I never wanted to stop listening. I'd pore over the Scriptures, highlighting the ones I felt God pressed on my heart. I started to replace harmful self-talk with God's promises that he loved me, cared for me, and would bring me into a spacious place. I resonated with the observation of Oswald Chambers, "Get into the habit of saying, 'Speak, Lord,' and life will become a romance."[11] This romance was life-giving and life-shaping, and I would never be the same.

But in my glee and wonder over hearing God, I rushed ahead eagerly and often got muddled, thinking that he was speaking to me when it was actually my own heart and desires talking. Eventually God used a major disappointment to spur me on to test more deeply what was and wasn't his voice. I needed to learn how to discern the tiny whisper of God through a relationship of trust.

I thought God had been thundering out his directions for my life, directing me to move to a certain city halfway across the country to a new job, where a man also happened to live whom I thought the Lord had promised I'd marry. But in the space of a weekend, both the job and the relationship came to nothing. My crushing sadness over these losses paled next to the sorrow I felt over not hearing God correctly. What was I basing my life on? What—or whom—was I listening to?

For a time I gave up trying to hear the voice of God. I felt too hurt that I'd been so wrong, and I didn't want to risk that again. But I missed the sweet intimacy I had enjoyed, and I longed to pour out my feelings to God and hear his loving words in return.

Slowly, tentatively, over the period of many months, I started again to share with God what was on my heart and mind. When I yearned to hear his still, small voice, I would tune in, hoping that I was really hearing him. This time I held the words tenderly, testing them against the wisdom of the Bible and sometimes sharing them with others who were mature in the Christian faith. I began to see that the romance of God's speaking could indeed be a daily reality, but I needed to be humble, open, and discerning.

Those who write about listening prayer and guidance suggest we test out what we hear from God with three helps: Scripture, impressions of the Holy Spirit, and circumstances. Dallas Willard adds our own judgment to the list, saying that sometimes God leaves it up to us to decide.[12]

We start to recognize the still, small voice with its gentleness but also its weight and authority. God's whispers speak right to our hearts if we open ourselves to hear him. His voice is unobtrusive, never overpowering. Of course, although God is infallible, we are not, and we should put on a robe of humility as we listen. We might hear God but fail to understand him correctly. Again, Dallas Willard: "The infallibility of the messenger and the message does not guarantee the infallibility of our reception. Humility is always in order."[13]

This is where community comes in. We need each other so that we can test out what we hear, weighing it carefully against Scripture and using our reason. We can also find help from those who've gone before us, such as a nun from sixteenth-century Spain. Teresa of Ávila shows us how to test whether we're hearing God's voice.

Practicing Discernment

Teresa of Ávila had an intimate relationship with God and, contrary to the authorities of the day, prayed to him from within herself (in what was known as *mental prayer*) instead of only through prayer spoken aloud in a group (known as *vocal prayer*). Because those in charge wanted to keep the faith pure, from their point of view, they deemed mental prayer dangerous. They even established the Inquisition to control the books that people read.[14]

For Teresa, hearing God's voice woke her up to his loving movement in her life. She whose mother died when she was young, who longed for maternal love and acceptance, who as a young woman got caught up reading literature of courtly love and forming questionable relationships, found the true Lover of her soul. As she heard his tender words of love, compassion, and affirmation, as she sensed the union with the three persons of the Trinity, she blossomed into a person who knew who she was—the beloved who sat at Jesus' feet.

As she grew in confidence in God, she realized she shouldn't prize messages from him for their own sake or puff herself up with pride over her closeness with him. Although vital to her spiritual journey, hearing God wasn't the most important thing.

Teresa gained the courage to work as a reformer, administrator, and leader. Without hearing God, she probably would not have set up new monasteries or penned her spiritual thoughts and letters. These twenty years of her writing can help us explore several of the key criteria she used to discern whether she and the nuns in her care were actually hearing God.

Authority

Perhaps one of the most important ways Teresa evaluated the words and messages she heard was through their authority. She explained that we can sense if we're hearing God when it seems we're listening to someone who is very holy or a person of respect, who we know won't lie to us: "For these words at times bear with them such majesty that even though one does not call to mind who it is that speaks them, they make one tremble—if they are words of reproof; and if they are words of love, they make one dissolve in love."[15]

God's words contain such power and majesty that we respond, whether through turning from sin or receiving his love. Teresa held a high view of Scripture: "Pay no more attention to those [words] that are not in close conformity with Scripture than you would to those heard from the devil himself."[16] She also trusted the Church as a source of authority and sought to obey it, seeing doctrine and the theological review of her writing as a means of determining whether what she heard was from God. However, as Teresa grew in confidence, she increasingly relied on her direct encounters with God over the authority of her confessors and censors.

Clarity and Certainty

Another means Teresa used to test what she was hearing was the clarity by which the words came and therefore the certainty she felt upon hearing them. As she wrote, "The certitude is so strong that even in things that in one's own opinion sometimes seem impossible . . . there is an assurance in the soul itself that cannot be overcome." The words from God are "never forgotten."[17]

Teresa said that words from God come unexpectedly[18] and quickly—too fast for us to make up on our own.[19] We cannot ignore them, "for the very spirit that speaks puts a stop to all other thoughts and makes the soul attend to what is said." After all, he who can stop the sun can make us stop and pay attention.[20]

The Source

Teresa had clear guidelines for discerning God's voice. And yet she still made errors in judgment, notably entering into an emotionally dependent relationship with a priest. How can we avoid letting our desires and presumptions taint God's words to us? After all, everyone has their own blind spots, and thus we need to continue to test out what we hear. When our emotions are involved, we must seek wisdom all the more. The biggest challenge in weighing the source tends to be figuring out if our own desires are speaking or if it's God (and of course, the two often combine, as God loves to work through our desires).

Another possibility, according to Teresa, was the influence of the devil. She longed that people would learn to recognize his work through experience, for although "his wiles are so many" and "he knows well how to counterfeit the Spirit of light," yet he cannot duplicate the good effects of words from God or leave the person with a feeling of peace and light. Instead, he leaves "restlessness and disturbance."[21] She counseled people to consult with someone they respected to avoid being deluded.

She also mistrusted abnormal supernatural experiences. She advised those experiencing extreme raptures and other phenomena to work hard to take their minds off themselves. For she knew that becoming more like Christ can be measured in loving one's neighbor. And she counseled humility, urging the nuns not to view themselves more highly than others: "Do not think, even if the [words] are from God, that you are better because of them, for He spoke frequently with the Pharisees."[22] She rooted her advice in common sense.

The Effect

Another key way Teresa assessed whether God had said something was through its effect in a person's life. For instance, true words bestow peace and calm: "the great quiet left in the soul";[23] they give a "spark of assurance."[24] She wrote from experience; as one who was highly strung and often anxious, she felt instant calm when God would say, "Be not afraid." Over many years she could trace the growth of her soul in maturity as she listened to him.

Another effect of the true words of God is the humility they impart: "The more [the soul] hears words of favor the more humble it should be." And "when the spirit is from God the soul esteems itself less"; she believed that "the greater the favor granted," the "more awareness [the soul has] of its sins and is more forgetful of its own gain."[25] As people become more like Christ, they become more aware of how they fall short of him because of their sins. And they seek his transformation all the more.

Some criticize Teresa today, saying that we cannot independently verify the ways she discerned whether she heard from God. But we see the fruit in her life. After all, *not* listening to God for fear that we'll get things wrong could close off an important avenue of spiritual growth. As we listen to and obey God, we'll change and become more like him. We'll gain wisdom as we weigh what we hear, and we'll increasingly embody the fruit of the Spirit as we follow Christ.

Prayer Practice: Praying with Teresa
Teresa loved the nuns in her order and wanted to teach them how to pray. Her book *The Way of Perfection* contains her grace-filled instructions to them.[26] Take some time to pray with Teresa, using her words to spur on your own conversations with God, perhaps choosing to focus on just one or two of these.[27] Following each prayer, I've included some bullet points to spark ideas as you converse with God and listen for his reply.

Finding Good in God
"Blessed are you, Lord, forever! You love me so much. What is this love that you have for us?[28] Do I love you, Lord? Are my desires acceptable in your sight? Oh my God and my Lord, deliver me from all evil and lead me to that place where all good things may be found. We have a living faith in what

the Eternal Father has reserved for us because his Son asks it of him. You, Lord, teach us how to ask."[29]

- Express your love to God and wait for his response.
- Talk to God about your desires; ask him to help you see any that have been hidden from you.
- Muse with God about the relationship between the Father and Jesus and the Spirit. What does God want to share with you about the Trinity?

Suffering

"You, Lord, suffered everything for me. What can I complain about? I am ashamed, Lord, when I suffer trials and don't count them as a great blessing. Help me take up my cross and not take heed of what others say. Help me to be deaf to all detractors. However hard my trials are and however deep my affliction, how much harder were yours and how much deeper your trials. What a weary journey you had to travel."[30]

- Share with God an experience that pains you, naming what you feel and why.
- Ask him to help you wait for wisdom about your situation before asking others for their advice. What words does he have for you?
- What does God have to say about how you're suffering? How does he respond to your pain?

Following God

"We get into trouble when we take our eyes off you, Lord. When we keep our eyes on you and watch where we're walking, we'll soon arrive; when we veer from the true way and remove our gaze from you, we stumble and fall a thousand times."[31]

- Tell God how you feel at this moment as you journey with him. Are you on the right path? Maybe you're veering off the path? Ask him to show you where you're walking and how he's with you.

God's Qualities

"You're our Ruler! You embody not only supreme power but supreme goodness. You're wisdom itself, without beginning and without end. Infinite are your works—I cannot comprehend them. You're a fathomless ocean of wonders; within you is contained all beauty. You're my strength. I cry out to you for help! Would I have the eloquence of the most learned and the wisdom of the most wise that I could describe your nature, our Lord who is good."[32]

- You might want to focus only on the first sentence of this prayer. Tell God how you feel about that and ask him to share with you what it means from his perspective.
- Spend some time using Teresa's words to praise God, naming his amazing qualities. Listen for how he receives your praise.

- Ask God to enlighten you about how you're made in his image. What qualities of his do you also therefore have? How might you use them for his glory? What does he say?

Although I got things wrong when I thought I heard God about that cross-country move for the job and the man, I'd never *not* want to listen for his still, small voice. I can't imagine life without a conversation with him—not only for his affirmation and love but for his inspiration, direction, and help as well. The humbling reminder of that time and others makes me cling to God even more and test what I'm hearing. As I grow in discernment, I delight when I sense him speaking to me, taking me on an adventure of love.

That time of sadness after I misheard God crippled me for many months. If I'd learned the language of lament, I would have been able to process my feelings in a more meaningful way. To this form of prayer we turn next.

5

THE PRAYER OF LAMENT

How to Cry Out to God

WHEN I WAS NINETEEN, one of my closest friends was killed in a car crash. Six months later another friend died from a brain aneurysm while hiking in Nepal. Seven months later my beloved grandfather died. I went from being an earnest but fun-appreciating college sophomore to one walking around in a daze. This extended period of grief overwhelmed me, and I responded by throwing myself into my studies and my part-time employment. During the summer I worked two jobs, six days a week, often going from the law office where I was an administrator to my evening/weekend work at an optician's. I tried to mute the stinging pain by staying busy. The feelings were still there, of course, but I tried to push them down and lock them up to keep functioning. I would, however, spend my lunchtimes at my friend's grave, eating a roast-beef sandwich from the fast-food chain Arby's while weeping over her birth and death dates. After that summer, I stopped going to Arby's.

We've all experienced horrible things like the death of loved ones and experiences that are awful but less piercing, such as a friend betraying us or a dearly held dream not coming to fruition. The reason is simple: We live in a world that is not as God created it to be. Because of the disobedience of Adam and Eve, our first parents, we've fallen short of our Creator's plan of life without disease, betrayal, broken dreams, or pain. Instead, along with the glories we experience, we endure those hard things, too.

We believe in a God who is both loving and almighty, one who could intervene if he desired. Perhaps he does—maybe he stops us from enduring a whole lot more pain than we do experience. We just don't know how much he saves us from. Yet when we encounter grief and bereavement, we often wonder where God is in the midst of it, since we know he's a good and loving Father. Has he abandoned us? Is he allowing this to happen—and if so, why? We may struggle to hear his voice and know that he's near.

During these times, the biggest leap of faith we may have to take is to cry out to God. When we do, when we share with him our pain and confusion, our anguish and heartache, we worship him through lament. Instead of backing away from God in bewilderment, we come before him face-to-face, approaching him with our pain. We offer this act of love and sacrifice as a prayer.

Perhaps we think that lamenting shouldn't be called prayer, for the word means "to complain, grumble, question, and protest." But the Bible is filled with lament. God's people don't shy away from complaining before him, as we see especially in the books of Job, Lamentations, and the Psalms (and note the obvious reminder of lament in the very name of the book: Lamentations). God welcomes our cries and doesn't tell us off for expressing our pain. We, in contrast, might have to give ourselves permission to let it out.

Praying with the Psalms

Our prayer book in the Bible, the Psalms, bursts with songs of lament, not only those written by individuals but those for use in corporate worship.[1] The psalmists cry out to God, asking and even demanding that he help them. Sometimes the authors complain about false accusations, persecution, or sickness. Sometimes they describe the trouble they face more generally. Usually at the end of psalms of lament, the writers come to a change of mood—they reach a certainty that the Lord has heard their prayers and will act to save them.

We see this pattern in Psalm 13, which starts off "How long, LORD? Will you forget me forever? How long will you hide your face from me?"[2] But the last stanza affirms the psalmist's trust in God: "But I trust in your unfailing love; my heart rejoices in your salvation."[3]

The psalmists most often move through their lament in

four stages: address, complaint, request, expression of trust. We see this pattern in Psalm 22.

Address

"My God, my God,"[4] David cried out, presenting his pain to his Creator. That he addressed God with intimacy invites us to do so similarly.

We might most associate these opening words—"My God, my God, why have you forsaken me?"—with those Jesus uttered on the cross. It's good to remember that David spoke them many centuries earlier to release his anguish.

Complaint

Why have you forsaken me?
    Why are you so far from saving me,
    so far from my cries of anguish?
My God, I cry out by day, but you do not answer,
    by night, but I find no rest. . . .

My mouth is dried up like a potsherd,
    and my tongue sticks to the roof of my mouth;
    you lay me in the dust of death.[5]

In the first two-thirds of this psalm, David detailed his complaints, sharing how forsaken he felt. He gave a sense of finality, as though he'd be cast out from the Lord's presence forever. These questions of why God seems silent while we endure deep pain can pierce us to the core. We share the sense of the complete abandonment that David voiced. That God would overlook us in our lowest moments feels even more of a slight, piling on the pain and bewilderment.

God's silence is so confusing—*Why*, we wonder, *won't he answer?* We can rail against him for the silence; we can shake our fists and cry in frustration. God doesn't smite us when we do so. Although he is God and therefore does not have to speak, he welcomes us to cry, mourn, and lament.

One way that David addressed the question of God's present silence was to point to God's mercies in the past: "You're the Holy One, the one our people praise. Those who've gone before us trusted you, and you saved them. They cried out to you, and you saved them."[6] David grieved that although God acted in the past, now it seemed he was nowhere to be seen. David didn't button up his pain but gave it to God.

Request

LORD, do not be far from me.
   You are my strength; come quickly to help me.
Deliver me from the sword,
   my precious life from the power of the dogs.
Rescue me from the mouth of the lions;
   save me from the horns of the wild oxen.[7]

We move to David's direct request to God. As he found himself in desperate circumstances, David made a succinct plea: "Don't be far from me! Come quickly and help! Deliver me! Rescue me! Save me!" David's cries for help were almost a reflexive response. We, too, when we face trouble, might feel the immediate need to take our requests to God, asking for his help. The more we train ourselves to turn to God in a crisis, the more natural it will become.

Expression of Trust

> Yet you brought me out of the womb;
>> you made me trust in you, even at my mother's
>>> breast. . . .

> I will declare your name to my people;
>> in the assembly I will praise you. . . .
> For he has not despised or scorned
>> the suffering of the afflicted one;
> he has not hidden his face from him
>> but has listened to his cry for help. . . .

> All the ends of the earth
>> will remember and turn to the LORD,
> and all the families of the nations
>> will bow down before him. . . .

> They will proclaim his righteousness,
>> declaring to a people yet unborn:
>> He has done it![8]

Though David accused God of being silent, in the psalm's last ten verses, he turned to praise as he expressed his trust in

God. Note how David was perhaps educating his emotions by saying, "I *will* declare . . . ; I *will* praise you."[9] He affirmed that God won't leave his people, that God hears them and meets with them. David knew that no matter what he felt, God was with him.

Address, complaint, request, trust. These four steps help our hearts and minds grapple with the pain we experience as we turn to, not away from, God.

Prayer Practice: Penning Your Song of Lament
Write your lament using the four stages outlined in Psalm 22:

- Address: How can you best address God in the particular circumstances that cause you to lament?
- Complaint: Tell God what you're feeling; don't hold anything back for fear of hurting or shocking him. He can take it.
- Request: Ask God what you want him to do. Tell him plainly and clearly.
- Expression of trust: Name what you believe about God's qualities, even if you don't feel your beliefs at the moment. You may need to educate your emotions, as David did.

Let's Look at Lamentations
The five lament poems in Lamentations are crafted to express the pain and torment of God's people. These poems, often attributed to Jeremiah, were written when the city of

Jerusalem was destroyed in 586 BC after the people had lived in the Promised Land for five hundred years. Under the leadership of King Nebuchadnezzar, the Babylonians broke through the city walls and plundered and burned the city, including the Temple. The city was laid waste, and the Temple desecrated.

With this act of war, the royal line of David was deposed and humiliated. As God's people were carried off into exile, they were bereft of their city and the Temple, where God dwelled. As they lamented before God, they accused him of not keeping his word to establish them in the Promised Land.

The five laments are tightly structured. Four of the five poems each have twenty-two verses to represent the number of letters in the Hebrew alphabet, and the other poem has sixty-six verses (three times twenty-two). The first four laments start off with successive letters of the Hebrew alphabet in what's known as an acrostic poem. Some Bible commentators see this structure as a way to control or contain the chaos of the deep anger, confusion, and pain Jeremiah felt.

God's people would read Lamentations on the anniversary of the destruction of the Temple, and today many Jewish people read it at the Western Wall in Jerusalem, the surviving remnant of God's Temple in the spot closest to the Holy of Holies. Many Christians read this book during the last three days of Holy Week.

Prayer Practice: An Acrostic Lament

Follow the form of Lamentations by praying through an acrostic poem of lament—you could write your own. Here's a sample (and yes, the letter *x* in *xenial* is tough!):

> *Actually, Lord, I weep.*
> *Because of the pain of loss, I feel destitute.*
> *Can I ever make it through this?*
> *Day by day I'm weary and worn;*
> *Everything is so hard and sad,*
> *For life hasn't happened as I had hoped.*
> *Great are my burdens and woe.*
> *How come you allowed this to happen?*
> *I can't hear you or sense your presence.*
> *Just let me know that you are with me;*
> *Keep me in the center of your love.*
> *Light my path, that I might again feel your warmth.*
> *Make me sure that you haven't abandoned me.*
> *No words can express my sadness fully;*
> *Oh God, please tell me why! Why?*
> *People say you're good, but I question that;*
> *Quite how you allowed this, I do not know!*
> *Right now everything feels bleak and gray;*
> *Simple pleasures have vanished in the mist.*
> *This time of sorrow seems never to end.*
> *Upon you, however, will I set my mind and heart,*
> *Voicing my worries and anxious thoughts while*
> *Welcoming your great mercies.*

Xenial I know you to be, welcoming me to your table,
You set a place for me even in my sorrow.
Zealous will I be about you; I praise you even now!

Prayer Practice: Seeing God with Job

Job is probably the person in the Bible we most connect to lament as he conversed with God even after he lost everything—his family, home, wealth, and health. He held on to his faith in God as he sought to find meaning in the difficulties.

Take a few moments and join Job in affirming that God is God—even in the midst of your pain. You might not feel the truth that God saves and redeems you, but as you pray through Job's words, God can help you receive an understanding of this reality in your spirit.

I've written a prose poem inspired by a passage from Job that you can pray through, or you could write, draw, or dance out your own version. Let his words lead you to lament but also, if you're able, to affirm that your Redeemer lives.

I know that my redeemer lives,
    and that in the end he will stand on
        the earth.
And after my skin has been destroyed,
    yet in my flesh I will see God;
I myself will see him
    with my own eyes—I, and not another.
    How my heart yearns within me![10]

I know, yes I know,
that the One who will save me
lives.
He lives;
he's not dead;
he hasn't disappeared.
Upon the earth
he'll stand one day.
One day,
at the end of time.

My skin may be destroyed,
not only by wrinkles
but through scabs and scars,
welts and wounds.

Yet in my body—
in my flesh—
I will see God.
I will!
Myself,
with mine own eyes!
I, not another.

How I yearn to see him!
My heart longs to behold his face.
Though I wither away,
yet I will see him.

So be it—
amen and let it be so.

Prayer Practice: Permission Slips

Some years ago, I grew close to an older woman who, with her husband, experienced a rags-to-riches success story. Her strength of will and positive outlook contributed to their attainment of wealth and social status, and she relied on her strong Christian faith to steer her. She was a great witness for Christ, but like all of us, she had some blind spots. In recounting how she and her husband weathered many storms, she always put an upbeat spin on the stories. With this determination to face the future positively, she eliminated any voicing of fears, questions, or pain. She refused to acknowledge any struggles that faced her. She never gave time to lament. Because of this, I didn't feel I could be fully honest with her. I felt stifled in my need and desire to express all of my emotions, even the untidy and difficult ones. It would have been wildly inappropriate given the dynamics of our relationship, but at times I wished I could give her permission to lament.

However well our lives are going, we all need to lament. We may think we're not supposed to feel sad about something, or that because we enjoy so many bountiful blessings, we really shouldn't indulge in what some call wallowing. Whatever the case, we can allow ourselves to lament through this simple exercise, which can have a profound effect. Simply write a permission slip that enables you to express your sadness, even if the matter feels trivial or if you think you shouldn't be grieving. You can follow up the permission slip with a prayer.[11]

Here's an example:

July 23, 2020. I, Amy Boucher Pye, give myself permission to grieve not being in Spain today because of the coronavirus pandemic. I wish we were at the beach today, hearing the roar of the waves or the fragments of Spanish or conversations in other languages. I wouldn't even mind being hawked the cheap sunglasses or massages. I'm disappointed that I'm not sipping a chilled drink while taking in the sun-kissed faces of those I love or feeling that amazing sensation of not having to be somewhere or to do something.

Even as I write, I realize I don't feel I *can* be sad about this. You've given me so much, Lord, that I feel I shouldn't complain. But I want to. I want to let out the feelings that I've buried inside, and I know I need your help to release them.

I realize that I want to stand up and scream or shake my fists at this horrible virus that has so changed our lives and affected so many people. I'm scared that my parents are going to get Covid; that I won't ever see them again. I'm disappointed that I won't be going to the States this summer to be with them. I'm angry and sad and fearful. Why haven't you intervened more? Why, Lord; why?

Lord, I don't understand all of the mysteries. And you know I feel bad about feeling bad about missing out on this vacation when others have struggled so much more than I have. But I give myself permission to feel this sadness nonetheless. I know you didn't create the world with disease. You didn't want your people to suffer and die. You even care about me missing this time in Spain and my planned trip to Minnesota. I give to you my feelings, all of them. Receive them and redeem them and deepen within me a sense of love, gratitude, and peace.

Prayer Practice: Praying at the Wall

Fiction can be a good way to experience the visceral feelings that lament expresses, such as *The Secret Life of Bees* by Sue Monk Kidd.[12] Her story about several sisters includes a practice based on Jewish pilgrims lamenting at the Western Wall in Jerusalem (which is sometimes known as the Wailing Wall because of how those who journey there pour out their hearts and prayers to God).

In the novel, May is the sister whose twin died some years ago. Ever since that tragedy, May seems to feel deeply the pain of others, so much so that it affects her health. Her sister August tries to get her medical help, but the doctors are stumped. All that seems to help her is setting up, as August said, "a wailing wall. . . . Like they have in Jerusalem. The Jewish people go there to mourn. It's a way for them to deal with their suffering. See, they write their prayers on scraps of paper and tuck them in the wall."[13]

When May experienced pain or heard of some kind of atrocity, she'd write what happened on a slip of paper and tuck it into the cracks in the stone wall that she'd formed. By doing so she experienced a sense of release.

We, too, can express to God our feelings of pain, hurt, disbelief, and anguish at a wall. This exercise can be done individually but also works well in a group, especially if you share afterward about how God met you during the experience.

Instructions

Find a wall to use as a place to express your laments. The kind of wall doesn't matter—I've led this exercise using the cracks in a concrete wall in Spain and a wooden fence in North London. After the exercise in North London, one of the participants said that he'd previously engaged in this prayer at the Western Wall itself, and beforehand he wasn't sure if the exercise would be as meaningful at "a fence in Finchley." But it was. God transcends our physical locations and will meet us where we're at, not only physically but spiritually and emotionally.

Use the wall as a conduit of God's mercy. Write any names or situations that you want to give to the Lord on slips of paper, and as you place them in the wall, know that God receives your prayer. Wait for any words, pictures, or verses from Scripture that he may have for you.

If you're doing the exercise in a group, have someone

remove the slips of paper at the end and destroy them without reading them to ensure confidentiality. As part of one retreat, we gathered to burn the papers; during another I put them in the compost, which gave us a wonderful image of the worms making something new and life-giving out of them.

Prayer Practice: Praying through the News
In the summer of 2016, I gave a talk on lament at our North London church. I'm struck now by the horrific list of what happened the month before I spoke: the acrimonious campaigning over the Brexit issue, followed by the divided vote; the killing of Jo Cox, a member of Parliament; the ISIS shooting at the Istanbul airport; the massacre at a nightclub in Orlando, Florida, fueled by homophobia; police shootings in Minneapolis and Baton Rouge, which sparked the killing of five police officers in Dallas; the atrocity in Nice, France, when a truck plowed into pedestrians in a terror attack; and an attempted military coup in Turkey that killed 265 people the day before my talk.

The news can be so awful that we can't even take it in, much less remember all the horrors that happened a few years ago. Yet other atrocities, including racially motivated killings, terrorist attacks, and natural disasters, remain indelibly etched in our memories. We might feel helpless and impotent over the state of the world, thinking that nothing we do will make a difference. But along with becoming a voice for the oppressed, we can lament before God. We can air our concerns and speak out our anguish to him on behalf of ourselves, loved ones, and strangers. We don't know how he'll answer our prayers and pleas, but in praying we affirm that he's our loving Father who hears us and sees us. We believe that he can and will act according to his purposes and plans—and his love for us.

For this exercise, open a news source on your web browser. Perhaps choose one outside of your political comfort zone and ask God to use any unease you feel as part of your prayers. Click or tap on an article that catches your attention. As you read through it, make a list of prayer points while offering them to God. Suggestions:

- Release your sorrow over what happened.
- Pray for the people involved, that God would help, heal, and encourage.
- Name any inherent evil, injustice, or bias, and ask God to intervene.
- Request that the Holy Spirit reveal to you why you were drawn to this particular article. Why did it touch you?
- Lift up any similar situations in your own life with your laments and requests.

Prayer Practice: Praying with Our Senses
When we lament, we can deepen the prayer by using our bodies, such as when we prostrate ourselves in grief. An exercise to engage our sense of taste can be done either individually

or in a group as we pray through the five main tastes—sweet, salty, sour, bitter, and savory.[14]

Gather the necessary items. Ensure proper hygiene, especially if you are doing this in a group, and if possible use five individual bowls per person, filling each with one of these ingredients:

1. salty: salt water
2. bitter: herbs, such as parsley or thyme
3. sour: segments of grapefruit or a cranberry or slice of lemon
4. savory: beef broth or miso (the fermented paste, diluted)
5. sweet: honey

If you're doing this on your own, pray through the prayers with the accompanying actions at your own pace. In a group, the leader will speak out the reflections and prayers and leave enough silence between them for you to wrestle with the prayers. (If you're leading the exercise, don't give in to the temptation of moving along too quickly.)

Take the bowl of salty water and dip your finger into it, tasting the liquid. God's people wept when Moses led them out of Egypt. Moses asked again and again, "Let my people go!" And Pharaoh would relent and give them permission to leave but then would retract it. The Israelites were trapped as slaves, weeping salty tears. As you consider the taste of salt, think about your own salty tears as you offer your hurts to

God. Pray also for all of the people who are enslaved today, whether physically, such as through human trafficking; emotionally, such as through an abusive relationship; or spiritually through following false gods. Know that God weeps when people suffer, and he weeps with you as you lament.

Next, chew some of the bitter herbs. For the Israelites, being enslaved in Egypt made them bitter as they were forced to work harder with fewer raw materials. The work was long, difficult, and physically demanding, and they let their anger fester into bitterness. Pray about any areas of bitterness you might harbor. How could God help you be relieved of this? Pray also about the bitterness that divides families, communities, and nations today, that God would make a way between warring peoples and enable true peace and harmony to develop.

Move to the bowl of sour fruit as you take a bite of what's before you. As the Israelites wandered in the desert, many of them wished to return to their lives in Egypt—even to their backbreaking lives as slaves. Their experiences of wandering left a sour taste in their mouths as they grumbled against Moses and against the Lord. As your mouth reacts to the taste of the tart fruit, pray about any areas of your life where you feel tempted to harbor sour feelings. Name the people, places, or situations, and if you're able, give them to God. Ask for his help for your heart to be released from your discontent.

As you taste from the savory bowl, think about God's command to the Israelites to offer sacrifices to him as a release from their sins: "Give this command to the Israelites and say to them: 'Make sure that you present to me at the appointed time my food offerings, as an aroma pleasing to me.'"[15] The wafting fragrance from the burning sacrifice would produce a pleasing, savory scent for the people and their God to enjoy as they humbled themselves before him. Then God sent his own Son, Jesus, to be the sacrifice for our sin: "Christ loved us and gave himself up for us as a fragrant offering and sacrifice to God."[16] Give thanks for this wonderful offering of God's Son, which confirms to us our identity as sons and daughters of the Father. As you taste the full-bodied flavor of the broth, ask God to help you not forget what it cost his Son to set you free.

Finally, move to the bowl of honey. As you taste it, enjoy the sweet sensation after the flavors of bitter, sour, and savory. Think about how God led his people into the Promised Land, "a land flowing with milk and honey."[17] The journey to inhabit the Promised Land was long and arduous as the Israelites faced not only powerful enemies but also their own lack of faith. But eventually they made it to the land and settled there. After the bitter experiences came a sweet taste of home. Commit to God your journey of faith and where you are in it, whether you're in the midst of hard and sour experiences or enjoying a period of sweet sensations. Ask God to give you peace and, if needed, forbearance and hope. Know that he promises to welcome you to the ultimate land of milk and honey, where he's prepared a place just for you.

Lament forms an important part of our prayers, helping us to be honest before God as we voice our disappointment and grief. It enables us to get in touch with our true emotions and experience God's peace and love as we share our pain with him.

We'll look next at another way of praying with the Bible that helps us access our deep emotions, often those we've buried. This time we'll put ourselves into the story through our imaginations.

6

ENTERING THE STORY

How to Pray with Your Imagination

AN INJURY LEFT HIM BEDRIDDEN, and with the days stretching into the nights, he turned to the only two books he had, one on the life of Christ and the other on the lives of saints. He wished he could read the stories that he usually preferred of noble knights and their conquests. He read and reread the books he was given, and when the reading became monotonous, he started to place himself in the stories. He'd alternate between imagining himself fighting a dastardly villain to protect the honor of a fair maiden and becoming one of the crowd following Jesus, watching in amazement as Jesus released a man suffering from demon possession. During the bedridden man's confinement, his imagination sparked to life, giving him a creative outlet and a shape to his days.

But he soon realized that his imaginings left him in different emotional states depending on which stories he entered—those of the royal court or those of Jerusalem and the surrounding areas. When he imagined himself the conqueror of battles, wielding his sword, he enjoyed the immediate intrigue but felt empty afterward. Yet when he imagined himself following Jesus, witnessing his healings and learning from his teaching, he felt inspired to give of himself. To serve others, putting their needs before his own. He realized that through this imaginative exercise, Jesus' teaching entered his heart and soul more deeply than it had before.

I'm speaking of Ignatius of Loyola (1491–1556), whose leg was shattered by a cannonball in battle. During his recovery he discovered the benefits of imaginative prayer using the gospel stories; he filled three hundred pages with his many notes on the life of Christ through placing himself into the gospel narratives.[1] This type of prayer later formed an important part of Ignatius's program of spiritual exercises for the men in his care. These were the first Jesuits, a Roman Catholic order that continues to this day, and gospel imaginative prayer (which I'll also call *gospel contemplation*) helps many people not only get in touch with buried memories and emotions but also deepens their faith in God.

Desire + the Holy Spirit = Transformation

Entering into a gospel story with our imaginations opens us up to the work of the Holy Spirit in different ways than when we rely on our rational minds. Receiving a truth directly, such as when someone speaks it to us, can be painful, and we might erect barriers to guard against hearing it. In contrast, when we use our intuitive and imaginative senses, we don't seek to control how we're praying. We can let our imaginations roam, asking the Holy Spirit to guide and guard us. By doing so we tune in to what Ignatius called "felt inner knowledge"—what we know through our hearts, not our heads; inner knowledge that is unique to us and known by God.

When we unearth our desires with the help of the Holy Spirit, we can be changed. We come to know what we're feeling and therefore understand ourselves better. God reveals our hidden feelings that we may have buried out of pain, shame, or negligence. As they are unearthed, we can move closer to God, speaking to him about what's going on in our hearts and minds and then listening for his response, the creative words that affirm our true selves. The wisdom and understanding we glean will be more intimate and profound than something another person teaches us.

The change comes through an encounter with the risen Christ, he who with the Holy Spirit lives and dwells within us. For in this type of prayer, we shift between engaging with the historical Jesus and the risen Christ. At one moment we ponder the man as we find him in the gospel story, and in the next, he comes alive as a living presence while we converse with him. He touches our desires, concerns, and fears as he reveals what may have been unknown to us. This movement between history and mystery is a prime gift of gospel contemplation.[2]

We encounter the risen Lord through conversation with him, which can come at any point as we're contemplating the gospel story. This time of discussion will probably be the most profound part of the exercise and might have a prophetic element as God touches us by his Spirit. How people converse will vary from person to person, with some enjoying a quieter contemplative approach and others having a more back-and-forth conversation. What's important is that we remain open to receive whatever God gives us. And, of course, that we discern whether what we hear is truly from God.

"But What about Me, Lord?"

One of the first times I tried out this style of gospel contemplation, I had been learning about Ignatius as part of some academic study. I longed that my studies wouldn't be just an intellectual pursuit, but that through them I'd encounter God. So one morning I put aside my assigned reading and followed Ignatius's instructions in his *Spiritual Exercises* for this kind of prayer.[3]

Before I share that experience, a few comments. One is that I feel vulnerable in sharing, for the exercise brought up some buried feelings that were hidden for a reason! You'll see that I interacted with the story by writing it out, but that's my personal preference and isn't required with this kind of prayer. Also, I'm including the text from Scripture as well as my engagement with it to illustrate how I interacted with God, because this dialogue with God—what Ignatius called a *colloquy*—is a key part of the prayer exercise. Thus I've included not only my prayers and thoughts but also how I sensed God replying in those moments. Discerning whether I'd actually heard God would be something I'd test out after the exercise.

The gospel story that I focused on was the foretelling of Jesus' birth as the angel Gabriel spoke to Mary in Luke 1:25-38:

> "The Lord has done this for me," [Mary] said. "In these days he has shown his favor and taken away my disgrace among the people."
>
> In the sixth month of Elizabeth's pregnancy, God sent the angel Gabriel to Nazareth, a town in Galilee, to a virgin pledged to be married to a man named Joseph, a descendant of David. The virgin's name was Mary. The angel went to her and said, "Greetings, you who are highly favored! The Lord is with you."
>
> Mary was greatly troubled at his words and wondered what kind of greeting this might be. But the angel said to her, "Do not be afraid, Mary; you have found favor with God. You will conceive and give birth to a son, and you are to call him Jesus. He will be great and will be called the Son of the Most High. The Lord God will give him the throne of his father David, and he will reign over Jacob's descendants forever; his kingdom will never end."

"How will this be," Mary asked the angel, "since I am a virgin?"

The angel answered, "The Holy Spirit will come on you, and the power of the Most High will overshadow you. So the holy one to be born will be called the Son of God. Even Elizabeth your relative is going to have a child in her old age, and she who was said to be unable to conceive is in her sixth month. For no word from God will ever fail."

"I am the Lord's servant," Mary answered. "May your word to me be fulfilled." Then the angel left her.

❧

Father, Son, and Holy Spirit. You looked at the world, filled with so many people, and those sinning so much. And you decided in your time—you who see and fill all time—that Jesus would become human to save the human race. Jesus would become man. And in the fullness of time, you sent the angel Gabriel to Mary.

Ignite my imagination so that I can see this happening, Lord. To compose this scene. To see the round earth with its many different races and the particular house of Mary and its rooms in the town of Nazareth in the province of Galilee.

Lord, all of those races and times. All of

those people. And there in the Holy Land, the Mediterranean world, is Mary. She's in her house—she's young. Are her parents around? Siblings? Is she alone? I've never thought about that—does Gabriel visit her with others around?

It's probably hot. Dusty. The sun is piercing, and she takes shelter inside.

And now, Lord, I ask for what I want—I ask for knowledge inside, interior knowledge, the gaining of insight and imagination from you who became human for me so that I may better love and follow you. Please, Lord, grant this movement inside of me by your Holy Spirit.

When Elizabeth is six months pregnant, you send Gabriel to Nazareth in Galilee. Little Galilee, often scorned. You send this angel to a young woman who is pledged to be married to Joseph. She's going about her daily chores, not aware that this day will change her life—and the universe.

Gabriel comes to Mary and says, "Greetings! You're highly valued! God is with you!"

Mary's stomach fills with anxiety at the sight of this angel. *What kind of greeting is this?* she wonders. Indeed, who is this, and why does he say that God is with her?

The angel says, "Don't be afraid! Don't fear! You've found favor with God. God's pleased with you! You're going to conceive and give birth to a son. You're to call him Jesus."

Mary is incredulous at his words. She tries to take it all in.

"He'll be great and will be called the Son of the Most High. The Lord God will give him the throne of his father David, and he'll reign over Jacob's descendants forever. His Kingdom will never end."

Mary can't fully grasp what the angel says. Her son, the Son of the Most High? The king who takes over the throne from King David? He who will reign over Jacob's offspring? The Kingdom that will never end? It's all too much, and she squeaks out a response:

"How can this happen? I'm a virgin, you know."

"The Holy Spirit will visit you. The power of God—the Most High—will overshadow you. The holy one born will therefore be called the Son of God. Here's something to help you believe— a miracle. Your relative Elizabeth, who has been barren all of these years, will have a child in her old age. She who everyone thought could never conceive is in her sixth month! No word from God will ever fail. You'll understand this when you see Elizabeth, full of new life."

Mary believes his words, or at least she wants to believe. She responds, "I'm the Lord's servant. Let it happen to me as you say."

And the angel leaves her.

Lord, I'm there at the scene. I can see that I'm Mary's sister and not Mary, for often I feel that the good stuff happens to other people. As the sister, I watch Gabriel come and speak to Mary. Part of me wants to be very happy for Mary, Lord, but part of me wants to yell and scream and ask why I can't be the one entrusted with a big gift. Why can't I have a big vision?

Why, Lord? Why don't you choose me? Why do I feel sidelined?

Beloved. I do choose you. I am not sidelining you. You feel overlooked. Even now, you feel like the sister who was silent and alone. The one disappointing your parents when they had to focus on others. But I was there with you, child. I wasn't overlooking you. I was seeing you.

Will I ever be Mary, Lord? Will I be the one entrusted with a big vision?

Child, I live in you. Jesus is born in your life. So much more than you can know. God is at work in you. The offerings you make are how I am born in your life. Know that there is safety in being hidden. I see you. I love you. Just follow me and know my love. That is enough. Trust me to do with your work what I will; trust me to take your seeds that you scatter and cultivate them in my Kingdom. I will guard those that I choose from the scavenging birds and the scorching sun. I will

*keep them from the encroaching weeds. This is my work,
not yours. Rest in my love and know that I am with
you.*

∽

I moved through this exercise with tears when I sensed that I
didn't need to feel sidelined and that God saw me, his touch
reaching a tender place within me. His love assured me that
I was valuable to him. I also understood that I didn't need
to worry and fret over how people would receive the stuff I
produced, for God would be the one to plant and water the
seeds. If and when some of those seeds died, I was not to
concern myself unnecessarily.

My time with this gospel story shows how I started off by
following the Scripture text closely and not adding too much
imaginative detail. Only after I worked through the text did
I allow myself to picture myself in it, as Mary's sister. Then
I got in touch with the deep emotions of feeling overlooked
and sidelined, and as I gave those emotions to God, he spoke
to me tenderly and lovingly.

God through Jesus and the Spirit showed me my desires
to be seen and heard, to make an impact with my writing and
speaking. In unearthing these feelings, he assured me that
he always saw me, that he was my main audience. He also
provided a gentle corrective when I realized that I shouldn't
be caught up in engineering a platform for my work; he
would use it as he wished. I began to trust him more fully

as I focused on sowing seeds and not on comparing myself with others or obsessing about my number of social media followers.

A few years after this experience, I'd forgotten what happened during the prayer time. In thinking about the exercise, I remembered that I had placed myself in the story of Mary and Gabriel, but only in trawling through my journals could I recall my feelings of being overlooked and my desires to be a main character in the story. Because God released me from the power of those feelings, I forgot them as I went about my daily life.

Limits and Fears

What could go wrong with gospel contemplation? Some Christians criticize imaginative prayer, saying that we are fallen and prone to errors and thus shouldn't trust our imaginations. The fear is that we'll "conjure up" something and attribute it to God. But although our imaginations can be overtaken with unhelpful images, we shouldn't let a fear of misinterpretation keep us from embracing this practice. We have the Holy Spirit to guide us, and we will find it most helpful to share what we experience with trusted friends who are mature in their faith. We need God's help in discerning not only this type of prayer but in using our reason to apply the Bible to our lives.

Others fear that a wrong view of God can distort imaginative prayer, such as if we see God as an angry despot, an uncaring creator, or a demanding father. Although these views of God will limit the exercise, this sort of prayer can actually be an antidote to the problem. When we reflect on the prayer exercise with a person we trust, we might begin to understand how we perceive God—and why. Our views can come out into the open instead of being buried and potentially exercising an unseen influence on us.

Prayer Practice: Entering a Biblical Scene

Why not give it a go? Following are instructions to put yourself in a gospel story or one from the Old Testament.[4] To imagine more easily, choose a story with action instead of one that focuses on Jesus' teaching. If you'd rather start with a guided example, skip to the next section.

Get comfortable and still yourself, asking God to help you shut down any distractions coming your way. Invite him to work through your imagination, that his Holy Spirit would fill you and direct you. That he would prevent anything from interfering that is not of him so that you enjoy freedom in the exercise. During your time of prayer, you might want to open your hands as a sign of receptivity.

How you enter the story depends on your preferences. For instance, if you can picture things visually, you might want to imagine that you're making a film. Or you might want to consider what sounds you would hear—the roar of the waves or the murmur of the crowd. Perhaps you do your best imagining through feeling the emotions, such as the incensed rage of the religious leaders or the desperation of the bleeding woman. Pay attention to the details—the sights, sounds, tastes, smells, and emotions. As you lose yourself in the story, meet Jesus there.

Remember that the aim is to encounter Christ, so try not to get distracted over the historical details—let God take your imagination to reveal something about yourself or him. And know that exercising your imagination takes practice. It might not come naturally at first, but through persevering you'll find yourself more able to engage. Most importantly, remember that God is with you—ask him through the Holy Spirit to guide you and spark your imagination. And know that God will honor your preferences and your personality as he meets with you.

Read through the Bible text a couple of times until you're familiar with the story. You might want to record yourself reading the story so that you can imagine freely while listening. Let the scene build up in your mind's eye and take time to see what is surrounding you, to hear any noises, to feel, taste, and smell. What is around you—where are you? Who else is there? What do you see and smell? What noises are in the house or on the street or wherever you are?

Who are you in the unfolding scene? You may start as a bystander, or you may be one of the central characters, or perhaps you play the role of yourself in the story. You may struggle here a bit, not feeling that you fit in. Know, however, that many different types of people may simply not be mentioned in the biblical text—women, children, onlookers, shopkeepers, and so on. Feel God's invitation to enter into the action.

Let yourself be drawn into the story naturally as you talk

with Jesus or another character. What's the mood? Joyful or tense? Confused or angry? Hopeful or quiet? Something else? As you observe the emotional state of those in the story, also note your emotions. How do you feel?

As you contemplate the story, you may wish to ask yourself the questions Ignatius posed:

- What have I done for Christ?
- What am I doing for Christ?
- What ought I to do for him?

Stay in the story as long as you choose to. Move into a time of talking to Jesus about what happened as you prayed and what feelings came up. If it's been difficult, express that. You may wish to ask him to reveal why it's been hard. As you come to the end of your time, commit yourself to God, giving thanks for his grace in your life.

You may want to write down some feelings, thoughts, and reflections after your time of prayer, noting how you experienced meeting Jesus and what you learned about yourself.

Here are some passages suitable for imaginative prayer:

- Matthew 14:22-33 (Peter walks on the water)
- Mark 10:46-52 (The cure of Bartimaeus)
- Luke 5:1-11 (Jesus calls three disciples)
- John 13:1-17 (Jesus washes the disciples' feet)
- Exodus 3:1-6 (Moses and the burning bush)
- 1 Samuel 3:1-10 (The call of Samuel)

Prayer Practice: Shining with Light

Let's move to a prayer exercise involving the story of the Transfiguration, when God the Father shone his light on Jesus. You can do this on your own or as a guided exercise in a group setting.

As you begin, know that you can take your time—God's not in a rush. Also, the Holy Spirit might take you in a different direction than the exercise goes. That's okay; follow the Spirit. You might want to read the story a few times to set the details into your mind and heart.

For a bit of context, remember that the Transfiguration occurred after Peter's declaration of Jesus as the Messiah, when the opposition to Jesus was building. In the midst of these tensions, Jesus told his disciples that he would have to go to Jerusalem to suffer many things and to die, and then be raised to life on the third day.

You may wish to open your hands in front of you in a gesture of openness. You could silently pray, *Father, Son, and Holy Spirit, I welcome you and thank you that you are with me. Quiet my heart and mind. Baptize my imagination, that I might receive your presence. Keep anything that is evil without and lead me into your kingdom of grace and love.*

Take a few moments to consider what you desire. What do you ask of God? What is on your heart right now?

Read Matthew 17:1-9:

After six days Jesus took with him Peter, James and John the brother of James, and led them up a high mountain by themselves. There he was transfigured before them. His face shone like the sun, and his clothes became as white as the light. Just then there appeared before them Moses and Elijah, talking with Jesus.

Peter said to Jesus, "Lord, it is good for us to be here. If you wish, I will put up three shelters—one for you, one for Moses and one for Elijah."

While he was still speaking, a bright cloud covered them, and a voice from the cloud said, "This is my Son, whom I love; with him I am well pleased. Listen to him!"

When the disciples heard this, they fell facedown to the ground, terrified. But Jesus came and touched them. "Get up," he said. "Don't be afraid." When they looked up, they saw no one except Jesus.

As they were coming down the mountain, Jesus instructed them, "Don't tell anyone what you have seen, until the Son of Man has been raised from the dead."

Begin to picture the scene in your mind's eye. Feel the sun beating down on your shoulders as you walk, the dust clinging to your feet. See Jesus taking Peter, James, and John up a mountain path. Imagine you're there with them and ask yourself who you are in the story. Maybe you are yourself, or one of the main characters, or a bystander. Feel your breath speed up as you fall in step with the others.

As you climb, spend a few moments focusing on Jesus. What does he look like today? How do you think he's feeling?

After what feels like a long time walking up the mountain, your legs aching, you reach the top, gasping for breath. You take in the view and gaze at Jesus, delighted to be in his presence. All of the sudden as you're looking at him, he's changed. His face shines like the sun, and his clothes are as white as the light. How does he appear to you? What does his face look like? As you witness this sight, what are you feeling and thinking?

As you're pondering Jesus so transformed, you see him talking with Moses and Elijah. What are they saying, if you can hear them?

Then you hear Peter talking to Jesus. You hear him say, "Lord, it's good for us to be here. I'll—if you wish—put up three shelters. One for you, one for Moses, one for Elijah." Why does he say that?

Peter's still speaking when a bright cloud covers all of you on the mountaintop. You hear a voice thundering from the cloud, "This is my Son, whom I love. With him I'm well pleased. Listen to him!"

As the words reverberate through you, you hear the disciples fall to the ground, terrified. How do you react? What's going on around you? What's Jesus doing? What emotions do you experience?

Then you look up, and you see only Jesus. He comes and touches the disciples. How do you want him to approach you?

Jesus then tells you all to stand up and not to be afraid.

How does he say this? What do you see when you get up off the ground, brushing the dirt and gravel off your hands?

You hear Jesus telling his friends not to share with anyone what they've seen until the Son of Man is raised from the dead. How do the disciples react to this command? How do you respond?

It's time to come down the mountain. You might be ready to make the journey down, or you might want to stay at the top a bit longer. How do you feel about returning to the activities of your day? Stay for a few moments in the scene, wherever you are, however God leads you.

As you come to the end of this time of imaginative prayer, you might want to read the passage from Matthew's Gospel again. You may wish to pray this prayer in closing:

> Lord Jesus, you were changed by your Father on that mountain. Thank you for coming to earth as a baby, living as a man, and dying for us. Thank you for your love poured out. Keep making yourself present to me, that I might know you. Help me live sacrificially as you did. And set in place whatever work you're doing, including what I've experienced and learned through this time of prayer. In your name I pray, amen.

Part of the Story

One day I led this prayer exercise with two close friends; with their permission I share how they engaged with the story. Notice how their experiences illustrate how unique each of us is and how two people can enter the story differently. Also note, if you're as wowed by their responses as I was, that each is a gifted writer with a strong sense of imagination.[5] We're not all made like that, but I trust God will work in and through your imagination in wonderful ways unique to you.

First, Tanya. When she imagined the scene, she knew that she was doubting Thomas; she had sneaked along uninvited and wasn't seen by the others. She felt that she was someone on the margins, someone who raised questions. As the events of the story unfolded, she evaluated and pondered each thing as it happened.

When she saw Jesus light up, she wondered what that was all about—was Jesus glowing from within like a light bulb, or was it a natural phenomenon like the sun shining all around him? *Maybe*, she thought, *there's a way to explain him lighting up; maybe it's a physical happening and not a metaphysical one.* She felt that she had the freedom to explore what was behind Jesus' change.

As the story moved along, she wondered about Moses and Elijah. She thought about how they symbolized the revelation of God through the Law and the Prophets, respectively, and how both went up a mountain at crisis points in their lives. Moses needed a word from God on the mountain to keep leading God's people, and Elijah went up the mountain when he thought he'd failed. As she viewed these Old Testament leaders from the vantage point of a doubter, she started to explore the question of whether Jesus similarly faced a crucial moment.

Tanya then connected emotionally with the story when she looked at Jesus and realized that he had been carrying many burdens. She had always previously interpreted Jesus' transfiguration as a story of comfort and reassurance for the disciples, but she saw now the possibility of Jesus needing reassurance himself. Jesus' humanity meant that he needed his Father's love and care. From this viewpoint, she realized that God's affirmation of Jesus set a pattern for God's affirmation of all who are burdened, which included her.

Knowing this, Tanya looked to how God would respond to her. She felt as if he winked at her, which made her feel validated. With that touch, she understood not only with her head but also in her heart that she wasn't an outsider or on the margins. God sees her, even when she feels invisible and unseen.

Tanya remarked that although she's a Bible scholar, she'd never before seen the story like that. Only in doing the imaginative exercise did she have this flash of insight.

Next, Amy. Reflecting on the exercise, she commented that when she engages with an imaginative exercise like this one, she remains herself and doesn't imagine herself as a biblical character. Because she has an active imagination, she finds trying to be a character in the story distracting because of questions of realism and authenticity—for instance, she would wonder what life was like for a first-century Jewish person. She would also find it tricky to imagine herself as a man, and if she could make that leap, she'd be more caught up in wondering what Peter himself would have been experiencing at that moment and not what Amy-as-Peter experienced.

So Amy was Amy, and as she and the disciples walked along, she saw Jesus pulling up a sprig of rosemary and rubbing it between his fingers. She thought, *He's so normal—look, he's doing what I would do in pulling up that herb. He's my friend. How, then, can he be the Messiah?*

When they got to the top of the mountain and she saw Jesus transformed, she thought she must have died and entered a heavenly vision because of how Jesus shone so brightly. Then when she glimpsed Moses and Elijah and supernaturally knew who they were, despite the bright light, she said to herself, "Yes, I'm definitely dead." *Moses is the Law and Elijah the Prophets*, she thought; *they represent strictness and story.* Yet in this heavenly circle of conversation, she could see how Jesus joined together the Law and the Prophets—and she was part of the conversation. *This*, she mused, *is what heaven is like.*

But she came back to earth with a bump when Peter made his statement about the shelters. *Well, I'm not dead!* was her first thought as she wondered what he was going on about.

When the big and overwhelming voice of the Father boomed out his words about Jesus, she realized that God was answering her earlier question about who Jesus is. Yes, he's a man who picks plants. But yes, he's also God.

Then Jesus approached the frightened disciples who were crouching down and told them not to be afraid. Coming over to Amy to help her up, he gave her the bit of rosemary he still held, telling her not to be afraid. She had the sense that this taste of heaven is where she's meant to be; her spirit is made for this. "So," Jesus said, "don't be afraid of this heavenly vision. There may be things to fear back down the mountain, but we'll deal with those things when we get there."

Later she thought about the herb and how rosemary symbolizes remembrance. How Jesus picked it up just as she was wondering about his humanity, and how he gave it back to her after the Transfiguration when she was considering his divinity. She knew that he could reveal to her layers of meaning even in something as ordinary as an herb growing along a path.

Prayer Practice: Step into the Gospels

Following is a list of ten of the fifty stories Ignatius featured in his *Spiritual Exercises* that you could enter with your imagination.[6] Using the previous guidelines from the section "Prayer Practice: Entering a Biblical Scene," choose one of the stories and put yourself into the action as you move between pondering the historical Jesus and encountering the risen Christ.

- The Nativity: Luke 2:1-14
- Jesus at the Temple, age twelve: Luke 2:41-50
- The temptations of Christ: Luke 4:1-13;
  Matthew 4:1-11
- The miracle at the wedding at Cana: John 2:1-11
- Jesus stilling the sea: Matthew 8:23-27

- Sending the apostles to preach: Matthew 10:1-42
- The raising of Lazarus: John 11:1-45
- The Last Supper: Matthew 26:17-30; John 13:1-30
- Jesus on the cross: John 19:23-27
- The ascension of Jesus: Acts 1:1-12

Ignatius lived a long time ago, but his ways to pray still resonate with so many people, in part because of how he helps us engage with Jesus. We've experienced how to do so imaginatively through the gospel stories. Next we'll turn to a way to pray that involves meeting with Christ as we look back over the events of our day.

7

REMEMBERING IN PRAYER

How to Move Forward by Looking Back

IN MY EARLY TWENTIES I met my friend Carrie in Athens, Greece, for a special vacation. Many of the details of our time together have sunk into the fog of memory, but some stand out these decades later. I can particularly remember those that Carrie encouraged us to write down when we listed our "highlights and lowlights" at the end of each day. Naming specific things we'd loved and not loved was a new practice to me, but one I enjoyed immediately. I can still recall that one of our lowlights in the Athens hotel was what we called the "puke-green wallpaper," and one of my highlights was walking off the plane and being immersed in the wall of warm air. Or the lowlight of arriving on one of the islands to hear the hotel didn't have our reservation, and the highlight of securing a lovelier hotel room for a cheaper price.

I've carried on the practice with our family vacations, and although our teenage kids often roll their eyes at the suggestion of doing it, after I start to list a few seemingly random things, they'll join in. What's so wonderful about this little exercise is how it focuses our minds on being specific and noticing not only what brings us joy but also what makes us sad, angry, or irritated. The more particular we can be in our list, naming unique things, the richer the memories will be later on.

I realized recently that these highlights and lowlights can morph into a prayer that helps me understand how I'm relating to God. As I pay attention in my life and look back, with his help, to name the things that brought me joy or frustrated me, I can understand how I'm moving toward or away from him. This type of prayer is often known as the *examen*, and it forms an important part of the spiritual program of Ignatius of Loyola, whom we met in the last chapter.

As we explore the examen and other prayers that help us look at our lives and our hearts in the presence of God, please don't think of these as sackcloth-and-ashes exercises of torturing ourselves over past sins. God's love will undergird any searching we do, and we can lean on him, asking him to guide us and stop us from digging up the things that will overwhelm us. I fully trust he'll answer this prayer—I've seen evidence of his grace in my life and in the lives of others. Change can be slow, but God is at work.

This way of praying forms another important tool for how we communicate with our Creator, the One who never stops loving us.

Ignatius and His Prayer of Examen

Let's look first at Ignatius's examen, for it's the self-examination prayer practice most recommended for us to incorporate into our daily lives. It emphasizes our freedom and desires as we follow Christ.

After Ignatius recovered from the cannonball injury—and from having his leg reset when the first time left him with a limp—he threw himself into the life of a disciple of Christ. Keen to engage in a program of spiritual disciplines to rid his soul of sin, he decided in 1522 to make a pilgrimage to Jerusalem from his native Spain. He stopped in the town of Manresa, and although he meant only to pass through, he stayed there for nearly a year, living in a cave.

He embraced a zealous regime of spiritual practices, including long periods of fasting, growing out his hair and fingernails, and other extreme things. He experienced times of both joy and contentment but also depression and anxiety. He started to despair that he'd never be free of his sins.

Then he encountered Jesus on the banks of the Cardoner River, and his life changed forever. As Christ opened his eyes and understanding, Ignatius grasped that Jesus was not merely a figure in history but a living Presence who would never leave him. For Ignatius, this was a key to a new way of living, and he abandoned his severe practices.

As he weighed his experiences, he saw how he responded to God and the stuff of life when, on the one hand, he was filled with joy and hope and, on the other, he experienced sadness, disillusionment, and despair. As he discerned how his feelings and emotions moved him toward or away from God, he named the first "consolations" and the second "desolations." He realized that a key part of the Christian life involves uniting our desires with the work of the Holy Spirit. As we figure out what sparks either consolations or desolations, we can more easily name those desires.

A Dynamic Prayer

Ignatius knew that the cares of the world can take over in our daily lives, but that special times away, such as going on a retreat, can make it easy for us to meet with God. Thus he developed a twice-daily routine to examine or weigh the conscience, which is where the name *examen* comes from. He advised people to pray at noon and at night and to follow a five-step approach of looking back over the past hours with the help of the Holy Spirit. Because this is a dynamic way to pray that sparks renewal and spiritual growth, Ignatius valued it highly. In fact, he urged those in his religious order, the Jesuits, to keep praying the examen even if they became too busy for other prayers.

When you're praying this way, remember that God will collaborate with you in it—as you dialogue with him about the events of the day, the Spirit will bring to mind memories and insights. We grow in wisdom and discernment as we understand how we respond to God. As we see how we move toward or away from him, we come to understand ourselves more as God sees us. And we can then embrace the freedom to live and love God and our neighbor.

Remember, too, that Ignatius designed the examen to open people up even more to God's love and release them into his service. This prayer is not a moralistic code set to constrain us but rather an exercise to encourage freedom and individuality as we seek to serve Christ. Because as Christians we need regular renewal, Ignatian spirituality calls for a daily practice of this prayer so we can cultivate a habit that promotes transformation. When we succeed—that is, when our desire for God so fuels us to embrace this practice regularly—we see our hearts, minds, and actions changed to be more like Jesus.

From an Accountant's Prayer to Conversing with God

Although Ignatius designed the examen to enable people to embrace freedom in Christ, Ignatian spirituality has at times had a moralistic emphasis. From the 1920s to the 1950s in America, for instance, many saw it as a way to count up the good and bad actions of the day—as such, it was known as "the accountant's prayer." Those praying it were given a booklet that outlined how to fight particular sins and faults; in that booklet, they were to document the wrongs they committed. The prevailing view of God was one of a "divine bookkeeper and stern judge."[1]

In Europe in the 1950s, sin was similarly counted but

with a military emphasis. Thus, Ignatian spirituality produced God's soldiers who viewed God as an eternal King who would subdue the world. This expression saw Christ seeking people to share not only the hardships and danger of the campaign but also the glory.[2] It emphasized the importance of obeying one's spiritual director.

In the sixties, the culture shifted and people on both sides of the Atlantic struggled with the moralistic approach. With this new era of openness, the role of the spiritual director moved from a "retreat master" to a shepherd or fellow discerner. And in the early seventies, an influential academic article recommended leaving behind the accountant's prayer to instead focus on our identity in Christ and how we move toward God or away from him.[3] This new emphasis focused on receiving God's love through a conversation with him about our emotions, beliefs, and behaviors.

Thus the prayer of examen returned to more of what Ignatius had in mind originally as people heeded his call to detect how God was moving in their emotions and feelings. The emphasis shifted from "Where have I followed or broken the rules?" to "Where have I met or not met God?"[4]

The Five Steps

As an overview, let's outline the original five steps of Ignatius's examen. I'll then share guidelines for you to pray it and explore its challenges and benefits, and I'll give some alternative ways of engaging with it.

1. *Give thanks.* To Ignatius, ingratitude was the root of all sin. When writing to a friend, he remarked that when we aren't grateful, we don't recognize the good things God gives us, which leads us away from God and into sinful behavior.[5] In contrast, giving thanks for God's gifts engenders a sense of wonder over his creation and helps us find God in all things, an emphasis for which Ignatius is known. We therefore start the examen prayer by offering thanks to God. We seek to feel gratitude with our whole selves, knowing that giving thanks helps us birth more desire for God.

2. *Ask for grace to know our sins and reject them.* Ignatius recognized the importance of petition; that is, of asking God for help to develop and be changed. Seeking God's grace reflects a partnership of love whereby God our Creator lovingly reveals our defects. This conversation between Lover and beloved doesn't morph into a dour and introspective time of beating ourselves up over our sins. Instead, we understand God as our loving Parent and not as a divine taskmaster or an uninterested deity. Even when we receive God's correction, we sense his boundless love for us. We thus can experience the consolations Ignatius spoke of because we know that God helps us understand our failings so that we'll love him more, become more truly ourselves, and serve others better.

3. *Give an account of our thoughts, words, and deeds.* This step involves moving through the day's actions and thoughts. We focus on the movement of our souls—how we reacted in various situations. For instance, when did we feel fear, boredom, joy, anger, peace, disgust, contentment? How did we move toward or away from God? Ignatius understood that the Holy Spirit brings to mind specific thoughts, responses, and reactions and helps us ponder these questions and gain in discernment.

4. *Ask God to pardon our sins.* Ignatius recognized that to experience freedom, people need forgiveness. He saw sin as "disordered attachments"—where our dreams, longings, hungers, and desires keep us from following God. When we name our individual sins and any unhealthy dependencies that come to light in the third step, we then ask God to forgive us.[6]

   In directing us to be aware of our sins, Ignatius sought to awaken us to their cost—namely, that Christ died for them. With this awareness, we can experience a deepening love for God and our neighbor. When we know that God truly accepts us—that he forgives us fully—we accept others as they are, forgiving their wrongdoing against us.

5. *Resolve to amend with God's grace.* In the fifth step, we collaborate with God further, looking back over the day just finished to discern our steps for the day to

come. As with all of the examen's points, we converse with God, talking with him about the hours that have passed and how we reacted during that time as we anticipate moving forward into the next day. Through this conversation we can uncover God's loving surprises that will release our creativity and spur us on to growth and change.

Prayer Practice: Let's Pray the Examen

Set aside just fifteen minutes to pray the examen. If you keep the time short and concise, you're more likely to pray this way. You might want to write out your prayers or speak them to God.

1. *Give thanks.* Turn your heart to God in thanks, naming specific things for which you're grateful.

2. *Ask.* Invite God to dwell with you through the Spirit and Son as you seek his strength, wisdom, and insight.

3. *Review.* Consider your words, thoughts, and actions and why you responded as you did. Where and when did you move toward God, and why? Away from him?

4. *Repent.* Ask God to forgive you for the ways you failed, and receive a clean slate through his love and grace.

5. *Renew.* While conversing with God, look forward to tomorrow, making plans for how you want to live as a child of God.

Benefits and Challenges of the Examen

Over the years, some have criticized the examen, saying that it sinks us into navel-gazing. But when we depend on God, the examen can actually release us from an unhealthy inward gaze and help us control our impulses. Through it God forgives our sins, and he challenges us, inspires us, and helps us love and serve him and our neighbors. Perhaps the most difficult part of the examen is losing interest in it when we're swayed by the competing priorities of life.

The benefits of praying the examen outweigh the challenges. One benefit is that this way of praying sparks change and transformation through its invitation to notice. We open our eyes to the wonders of God's world, seeing his fingerprints not only in creation but also in ourselves. We come to see ourselves as God knows us.

Becoming open to God might mean delving into memories or feelings laced with hurt or bitterness. We might naturally avoid these places of pain and keep locked away our feelings of guilt and inadequacy, our memories of failure, or our sense of shame. But when we bury these emotions, the undercurrent can pull us in unwanted directions. Better to let the affections surface and bring them to God, often with the help of a trusted friend, to dilute their power.

Another benefit of a regular practice of the examen is that it helps free us of the effects of unconfessed sin as we become more aware of our potential for being deluded or swayed from God's way. Our conversations with God will help us discern what is true and right and what is not. As we're aware of our sin, we'll become increasingly humble and open to the needs of those around us.

The examen can also become a means of release, inspiration, and discovery of our true identity. This identity is what the apostle Paul spoke about in many of his letters—leaving the old self behind and embracing the new self. The verbs Paul used indicate that this is an active process.[7] Ignatius's examen is a means of heeding Paul's advice, for a new self is born when we give thanks, name our sins, receive forgiveness, and hear and heed God's invitation to follow him. We put on the mind of Christ and become characterized by the fruit of the Holy Spirit.[8] We'll grow in wholeheartedness, an inner stillness and peace, and a newfound reservoir of courage.

With the examen we'll also enjoy a new sense of spontaneity through the inspiration of the Holy Spirit. We'll become more sensitive to discerning God's voice and moving forward with him as we reject the call of the things of the world, our sinful desires, and the evil one. We'll increasingly discern the presence of the risen Christ and the Holy Spirit, who take us to the Father.[9]

Prayer Practice: Two-Pronged Questions

Ignatius always emphasized an individual's freedom, so if you find praying the five-step examen too formal or monotonous, or you struggle to incorporate it into your daily life (I'm no stranger to this!), feel free to experiment with what works best for you. You might, for instance, want to use the practice to focus on one area of your life, as exemplified in the prayer practices in the rest of this chapter.[10]

Here are some questions you can consider not only at night but at various moments in the day. Ponder them with God, asking for insight and wisdom.

- For what am I most grateful today?
- For what am I least grateful?

- When did I feel most alive today?
- When did my energy drain out of me?

- When today did I most feel like myself?
- When did I feel most disjointed?

- When was I happiest?
- When was I saddest?[11]

- What brought me joy?
- What annoyed me?[12]

Prayer Practice: An Important Person

Pray about a particular person and the relationship you share.

1. *Give thanks.* Begin by thanking God for something you've noticed today or something that happened. Perhaps it's a way that you responded to someone.

2. *Ask.* Ask God to show you one person you can focus on in prayer during this time. A name or face might come

to mind immediately if you've been thinking about this person a lot. Or you might want to wait a few moments to discern which person to pray about.

3. *Review.* Consider how you are with this person. What two or three words would you use to characterize your relationship, and why? How does this person help you move toward God? Away from God? Picture moments together—conversations, experiences, shared projects. How do you act when you're with this person, and why?

4. *Repent.* Name the ways you've failed this person, asking God to cleanse you from your wrongdoing. Be specific as you list hurtful words or ways you've let this person down. If appropriate and safe, you could write a letter or plan time for a talk to confess your failings and ask for forgiveness. Spend time receiving God's forgiveness.

5. *Renew.* Imagine how you could bless and love this person. What good things could you do together for leisure or service? How could God use you in this person's life? How could you help them to be more the person God has created them to be?[13]

Prayer Practice: The Work of Our Hands
Pray about the work God has given you to do.

1. *Give thanks.* Start off with thanking God for how he's made you as a person, for your unique blend of gifts,

passions, talents, and experience and how you express that through your work.

2. *Ask.* Set before God your work, whether or not it involves paid employment, asking him to illuminate your feelings about it. Ask for insights and wisdom regarding how you contribute to God's world.

3. *Review.* List the various components of your work and evaluate with God which ones are necessary and which you might be able to release. Which parts of your work make you feel most alive? Which drain you of energy? How are you using your gifts in this work? Do you feel fulfilled or thwarted or somewhere in between?

4. *Repent.* With God's help, name some things you've gotten wrong with your work. Which people have you let down, and why? What judgments did you make that ended up affecting someone else adversely? In which ways does your work make you complicit in institutionalized evil? After repenting, receive God's forgiveness. You might want to release the sins symbolically; if you jotted them down on a piece of paper, you could burn or shred it.

5. *Renew.* Dream with God about how you could use your wisdom, experience, and passion in your work. What relationships come to mind? What have you left undone that you're keen to get going on? What

world-changing dreams bubble away in you? Commit not only to dreaming but also to working with God to see if you can make some of these happen.

Prayer Practice: Praying for the World

Our world faces many challenges—political unrest and division, natural disasters, diseases, inequality, and so on. The list is long and can feel overwhelming, but God cares for us and his world and welcomes our prayers about it.

1. *Give thanks.* Name some of the wonders in God's creation that you're especially grateful for—places, foods, types of plants and animals, a stunning sunset. Spend some time delighting in these good things that God gives us, listing them one by one.

2. *Ask.* Invite the Holy Spirit to partner with you in praying for God's world. Ask for help in focusing your prayer on one particular concern.

3. *Review.* Pray through the issue as best as you can, naming some of its inherent challenges and asking for God's intervention. Think through why the situation has reached the point it has.

4. *Repent.* Name the ways you may be complicit. How have you added to the problem? Ask God to reveal any ways you've contributed, especially if they are hidden to you. You can also repent on behalf of a group

of people, asking God on behalf of others to release forgiveness. Seek his grace and love for the situation.

5. *Renew.* Focus on how God brings redemption—how he can bring beauty from ashes. How might the Spirit spark change and renewal in this area? How could you be part of that? Are there specific things you could do to bring transformation? Dream also about how God could bring change on a level outside of your involvement. Resolve to act as the Spirit inspires you.

Pray with John Wesley

A man who lived two centuries after Ignatius also pursued holiness through a daily prayer of self-examination—John Wesley (1703–1791), the English founder of Methodism. He was raised by his parents, Samuel and Susanna, a clergyman and his wife who sought holiness through a strict regimen of rules for living.

Wesley embraced a highly disciplined routine, not only from the influence of his parents, but also because of his disposition. Like Ignatius, he was influenced by reading Thomas à Kempis's devotional work *The Imitation of Christ*. After reading it, Wesley offered his will to God and sought to glorify him. He created a prayer for self-examination in 1729 at Oxford when he developed twenty-two questions that he and a group of friends used daily. (They used these questions "methodically" to be accountable spiritually, which eventually birthed the Methodist movement.)

Wesley emphasized the need for direction and discipline in response to God; his questions are thus peppered with specific areas of holiness to explore. As Methodism grew, Wesley encouraged different shades of examination—self-examination, family assessments, home visits—to aid the pursuit of holiness.

His prayers of self-examination are no longer used widely, even by Methodists. Some people find a daily praying through these questions laborious, and others say the process could turn one's focus too inward. But praying through the questions on a retreat or quiet day can be a helpful exercise.

Prayer Practice: Wesley's Questions

Most of Wesley's twenty-two questions appear in a yes/no format, which can feel stark and limiting. I've adapted some of his questions into a more open-ended format. Pray through them, asking God to bring to mind your answers so that you can be made more like him. Do so knowing that God surrounds you with his grace and love.

- How's my impression management? How often do I create the image—consciously or unconsciously, online or in person—that I'm better than I really am? Why might I do this, and how might God help me in it?

- How am I doing with keeping things confidential and being a person who can be trusted?

- How often do I engage with some key spiritual practices, including reading the Bible, praying, and sharing my faith?

- What does my conscience tell me? What do I need to pay attention to here, and why?

- How am I acting toward others—how often am I jealous, critical, irritable, touchy, or distrustful?

- How is my relationship with God? Am I listening to him and obeying him?[14]

Keeping a Prayer Journal

A journal can be an important place for us to examine what's going on in our hearts and minds. Indeed, we may wish to use a prayer journal as we pray through the examen.

I kept a journal for many years, but early on it was an angry place where I came mostly to spew out my disappointment, hurt, and fears. Then I learned about keeping a prayer journal in which I wrote out my thoughts, feelings, and dreams in the form of prayers. I could still vent, pouring out all that weighed me down, but now I expressed those feelings to God. I also jotted down how I sensed he replied. Instead of the journal being a one-sided thing that left me spiraling down even more, it became a safe place in which to talk with God. There he would assure me of his love; there he would spur me on to love and good deeds.

After a few years of this practice, I realized that looking

over my collection of prayer journals gave me insights into my life with God. I could see the movements of my soul while tracing how I responded to God and to what was going on in my life. I began a once-a-year practice of reviewing my prayer journals as a form of the examen prayer.

I would set aside some time to note highlights and low-lights, and in doing so I saw not only how I sensed God's presence, wisdom, and direction but also what was happening with my emotions, family, friendships, and work. The journals bring back memories I may have forgotten, but more importantly, they reveal my relationship with God.

Yet life can become crammed with many things, and I can get out of sync with what forms an important practice for my spiritual well-being. In early 2019 I went away on a retreat, fortified by the amazing views of the Yorkshire countryside. I knew I was a bit behind with reviewing my prayer journals, but I experienced a jolt when I realized I had to start reading my journals from 2015! I had four years to read because in the previous years I'd pushed myself so much with writing and speaking, delving into my master's degree, and the family joys and traumas that had filled my days and nights. That I had so neglected this practice told me that my priorities were out of whack, and I needed to change. I did so not out of guilt but by seeking God's inspiration. I found the journey enlightening as I was reminded of his great mercies, love, and care.

If you keep a prayer journal, consider incorporating a monthly or yearly review. To do so, you could reread your journals and make notes, staying aware of various areas of your life, such as your relationship with God and with others, how you're doing emotionally or physically, and how your work/school/volunteer projects are going.

I like to create a yearly summary document that consists of the highlights from each month. This is something manageable that I can read and reflect on as I ask God not only to show me how I'm moving toward and away from him but also to remind me of how he's poured out his love in my life. Once a decade you could then read through your collection of summaries from each year of the decade as you remember God's grace and seek his illumination.

Looking back over a period of time helps us to discern how God is working in our lives. As we notice his fingerprints, he awakens us even more to receiving his nudges of grace. Whichever practice of examen best fits you, I hope you find one that helps you look back to move forward.

Afterword

Prayer: An Adventure with God

As you've seen, I'm pretty excited about prayer. Prayer changes people because God changes people. He takes those of us who are scared, anxious, bitter, disappointed, and vindictive and morphs us through his Spirit into brave, loving, hopeful, generous people. I've experienced his transformation, and I've witnessed it in those I love.

Take my parents, Phyllis and Leo. They are quiet, unassuming folks—both grew up on farms in the Midwest and are no strangers to good, hard work. But Leo's transformation through prayer was rather spectacular.

The Communion of Saints

The second of four kids living in rural Minnesota, Leo faced a massive life change when he was nearly eleven. One

Wednesday his gentle giant of a dad, George, went to help some neighbors with the harvest, as they'd come down with a strange virus that caused painful muscle aches. By Saturday night, George died from polio.

The once-solid foundations of Leo's life crumbled. The devastation of his father dying brought about in him a profound insecurity and a crippling fear of death that permeated his life for nearly three decades. His family plunged into deep poverty. His mom had been solely dependent on George—she didn't know how to drive a car or run the farm and knew nothing about the family finances. George hadn't had any life insurance, so there was no relief in that. And there was no support from the government. But they didn't starve because they had the eggs, potatoes, and milk from the farm.

Over the years Leo's anxious childhood exacted a toll on him. Looking back, he paints the picture of a man eaten away by fear and worry. "Before God did major work in my life, I was cheap—afraid to spend money because I had been so poor when I was a child; I couldn't really talk to friends or relatives; I was afraid of authority at work, terrified to give a talk or lead a discussion, too self-conscious to sing in church, rarely prayed, was dependent on tobacco, had an instinctive fear of and even hate for strangers, was often anxious and worried, and had a great fear of death—mine or someone in our family."

But in Leo's midthirties, God began to change all of that. "It started with a dream. In it I was at a retreat, and most of the people there were strangers to me. For some reason we knew that this was going to be a very special time. We gathered in a large group and were each given a sheet of paper with a short prayer at the top, followed by a long list of our faults. We were then going to find out the one thing on that long list that was our major problem in life, which the Lord would completely fix. This problem was the one thing that most kept us from coming closer to Christ.

"I didn't even read the prayer on the top of my paper but noticed immediately that the third item was printed in bold type with large letters: **SCARECROW = AFRAID OF PEOPLE!** I felt sure that others could see this, and I wanted to hide the sheet of paper. But I knew that after we prayed together, the Lord would completely fix this problem.

"Then the radio on our alarm clock came on, and instead of this wonderful experience of the problem being fixed, I had to get up and go to work. But I had the sense of how fast and easy it would be to make a major change."

The new pastor at my parents' local Catholic church played a crucial role in my dad's transformation.

"Father Tony introduced a new Sunday-night course called the Christian Life series. He adapted material from Catholic Pentecostals, along with some from evangelicals, like the four spiritual laws—we needed to renounce our sins. The music and songs were from the Southern Baptists.

"What we learned is that God was not just a judge, judging us, but that he loves us and that we need to respond to his love on a daily basis. During one of the sessions, we asked the Holy Spirit to fill us completely so that we would be immersed in the presence of God.

"After this prayer, in the service afterward, I had a vision only a half second long." This followed on from Leo's dream from several weeks before. "In the vision I saw Jesus like a huge light, and we all were like small lights around him—think of the sun with us as stars. We were all the very best friends and knew everything about each other, even our faults. But Jesus was forgiving all those faults and our sins, and we were all so happy. We were saying to each other, 'Isn't he wonderful! Isn't Jesus wonderful!' I cannot put into words how amazing it was.

"And even our sins and faults were being redeemed by the Lord, with beautiful shades of color shining out of everyone. To get an idea of this communion of friends, think of your very best friend—perhaps someone you have known for many years. Think of having complete transparency with this person; you know their good and bad points but are totally accepting, and the reverse is also true. Now imagine a third person, a fourth, and so on—all in this intense communion of mind and heart. Finally, imagine being in a crowd of hundreds of thousands, all who are being loved and redeemed. That's what it was like. After that half-second vision, I was no longer afraid of people. I couldn't be because I could see how Jesus loves and forgives all of us." As Leo ruminated on the vision, he realized that it points to the mystical communion of the saints: "This is the connection between people that goes on all the time although we don't see it; we'll see it after our death."

After this vision, Leo was released from his fear of people. And his view of God changed too. No longer was God a powerful but distant star as he used to see him. "Now I think a better image is that of God within us like a star. He is always polishing us, taking off the dark so that light can shine through us. And the light comes out in various beautiful colors, a different set for each person."

A Daily Softening

Phyllis, in contrast, is a bit more wary of visions and dreams, and God honors her preferences. Regular, daily intercessory prayer has birthed in her the fruit of the Holy Spirit, such as being loving, gentle, trusting, compassionate, and caring.

Some years ago we faced some family circumstances that were dire, troubling, and worrisome. The kind you can't change through force of will or action. The kind that "can come out only by prayer."[1] Mom, a real doer, felt helpless. Out of a sense of deep love and perhaps an undercurrent of desperation, she turned to prayer. She decided to fast between meals, not enjoying a single sample of cheesy pizza from Costco or a muffin with coffee when out with friends. When her stomach growled, she prayed. And she prayed when it didn't. Then Dad joined her in the fasting between meals, and some serious powerhousing prayers were going on in their patch in Minnesota.

After some months, in an amazing turnaround, the situation got sorted out over one weekend. We were grateful and relieved, and I attribute the change to God responding to those many prayers.

An unexpected bonus of the prayers has been the continued shaping of Mom to be more like Jesus. The crisis is behind us, but new ones arise and she keeps on praying, keeps on fasting, and keeps on being transformed by the Spirit. The change is clear—she's more trusting, more filled with peace, more free in showing empathy and love.

In our weekly calls, I share the things I want my parents to pray over, knowing not only that they will, but that our Father in heaven will hear them and respond with love. And he'll continue to change us all to be more like him.

Powerful Prayer People

I know we don't all have amazing parents like mine, and you might read my story with a tinge of sadness if you haven't experienced such an outpouring of love. But our God is a God of abundance, and he can send you some adoptive parents or grandparents or wise friends who might be older or younger than you are and who will pray for you. Who will support you and be cheerleaders for you. Who will be the hands and feet of Jesus in your life.

You might have to initiate your own group of prayer buddies. For instance, four of us like-minded women chat most days on a social media messaging service as we share with each other our needs, big and small. If I'm speaking at a Christian gathering, I know these women are praying for me through the day, often hour by hour. If one of their daughters gets married, as happened recently, we pray through the travel arrangements and practicalities surrounding such a joyous occasion. For another, an impending house move has been filling her mind and heart, and we're praying for just the right place for her to live.

I also have a slightly larger group of people who pray for me and my family. I often quote Alfred, Lord Tennyson, and his words apply to them as well: "More things are wrought by prayer than this world dreams of." We simply don't know how God answers our prayers. Maybe heaven will be a place where those questions are answered. Maybe we won't need to know how God answered the cries of our hearts, but perhaps he will delight in showing us.

Might you develop a group of people to pray with and for? In doing so, how could you employ the wonders of technology, such as video chats, text-messaging services, and so on? It can feel vulnerable to ask others to join us, and overcoming the technological challenges can feel difficult or intimidating, but I know from experience that you'll be hugely blessed if you pursue this.

The Carpenter's Plane

May you enjoy the adventure with God that is fueled with prayer. My hope, which is supported by a strong faith and belief, is that God will meet your deepest needs as you reach out to him in whatever ways you prefer, whether the seven ways we've explored or others. May he surprise you and delight you; may he work through you to spread his love and life to others.

May you meet the Carpenter as he planes off the rough edges and waits patiently for you, in the words of one of my dad's favorite prose poems:

> But every desire we have for [God]
>   and every prayer
>   is like the stroke of a [carpenter's] plane
>   that thins down our wooden-hearted incredulity;
> and when we've prayed enough
>   and the boards are worn quite through,
>   we'll realize God was there all the while,
>   waiting patiently,
>   pressing hard to set us free.[2]

Acknowledgments

Any book baby is born only with the help of many. I'm sending a huge thanks to:

Those who pray for me regularly; you're spread around the world and are a gift that keeps on giving. My texting friends—Ali, Anne, and Julie—thank you.

Tanya and Amy, with whom I've chatted weekly via video link before Zoom became all the rage. You see me and cheer me on; you help me find my words and my voice.

My early readers, who encouraged me, spotted errors, and helped me know when to press Delete: Ali Grafham, Bill Haley, Tony Horsfall, Anne LeTissier, Cathy Madavan, Barbara Schultz, and last alphabetically but not least, Sheridan Voysey.

Two of my wonderful tutors from my time at Heythrop College, University of London, from whom I gained so much. To Edward Howells for his insightful comments on Teresa of Ávila and to Gemma Simmonds, CJ, for her feedback on the chapters on Ignatius of Loyola.

My friends at NavPress and Tyndale—wow! Don Pape, for your enthusiasm for the project while you were publisher at NavPress and for helping clear the way for a smooth relationship.

Dave Zimmerman, your words are apt: *you're* awesome. Massive thanks for shaping the form of the book. Throughout the writing and editing process, you've seen what I've wanted to do, even when I couldn't yet articulate it; I'm thankful indeed. Jennifer Lonas, for working your copyediting wonders, in concert with Elizabeth Schroll, and Olivia Eldredge for managing the editorial process so well. I'm grateful, David Geeslin and Kristen Schumacher, for your marketing and publicity work in getting the word out, and Ron Kaufmann for your design. Thank you, too, to Elizabeth Neep and the team at SPCK, my British publisher.

My family, here in London and abroad. The gestation period of this book coincided with my hip replacement and the various lockdowns of the coronavirus pandemic, but we're making it through with grace and love. Thank you for spurring me on, serving me, and keeping me going.

For Further Reading

PRAYING WITH AND THROUGH THE BIBLE

Casey, Michael. *Sacred Reading: The Ancient Art of* Lectio Divina. Liguori, MO: Liguori/Triumph, 1997. This was the first book I read on *lectio divina*, and it influenced me the most; I recommend it as an initial port of call.

Johnson, Jan. *Meeting God in Scripture: A Hands-On Guide to* Lectio Divina. Downers Grove, IL: IVP, 2016. Forty exercises of *lectio divina* from a trusted guide.

PRACTICING THE PRESENCE OF GOD

Brother Lawrence and Frank Laubach. *Practicing His Presence.* Auburn, ME: Christian Books, 1973. I like this approachable translation. For a more precise version, with a wonderful introduction by Jennifer Rees Larcombe, see Brother Lawrence, *The Practice of the Presence of God.* Translated by E. M. Blaiklock. London: Hodder and Stoughton, 2009.

Cassian, John. *Conferences.* Translated by Colm Luibhéid. Mahwah, NJ: Paulist, 1985. An introduction to this early Christian and his formula for unceasing prayer.

HEARING GOD

Greig, Pete. *God on Mute: Engaging the Silence of Unanswered Prayer*, rev. ed. Grand Rapids, MI: Zondervan, 2020. The best book on when God appears silent. Also don't miss his accessible guide based on the Lord's Prayer: *How to Pray: A Simple Guide for Normal People.* Colorado Springs, CO: NavPress, 2019.

Willard, Dallas. *In Search of Guidance: Developing a Conversational Relationship with God.* San Francisco: HarperSanFrancisco, 1993. Later released as

Hearing God: Developing a Conversational Relationship with God, rev. ed. Downers Grove, IL: IVP, 2012. The best book on hearing God.

Williams, Rowan. *Teresa of Ávila*. London: Bloomsbury, 2003. An approachable introduction to this wonderful woman of God.

THE PRAYER OF LAMENT

Billings, J. Todd. *Rejoicing in Lament: Wrestling with Incurable Cancer and Life in Christ*. Grand Rapids, MI: Brazos, 2015. A scholar writes movingly and winsomely about life in Christ and his incurable cancer. A stunning book.

Vroegop, Mark. *Dark Clouds, Deep Mercy: Discovering the Grace of Lament*. Wheaton, IL: Crossway, 2019. A deep dive into the scriptural basis for the practice of lament from a pastor marked by a bereavement.

IMAGINATIVE GOSPEL PRAYER

Munitiz, Joseph A., and Philip Endean, trans. *Saint Ignatius of Loyola: Personal Writings*. London: Penguin, 2004. The gold-standard translation of Ignatius's works, with an introduction.

Oestreicher, Jeannie, and Larry Warner. *Imaginative Prayer for Youth Ministry: A Guide to Transforming Your Students' Spiritual Lives into Journey, Adventure, and Encounter*. Grand Rapids, MI: Zondervan, 2006. Although this resource is designed for youth ministries, you could easily adapt its interactive prayer activities for your own use.

THE PRAYER OF EXAMEN

Gallagher, Timothy M. *The Examen Prayer: Ignatian Wisdom for Our Lives Today*. Chestnut Ridge, NY: Crossroad, 2006. A rich and engaging exploration of the subject.

Manney, Jim. *A Simple Life-Changing Prayer: Discovering the Power of St. Ignatius Loyola's Examen*. Chicago: Loyola Press, 2011. A bite-size but helpful introduction.

Notes

INTRODUCTION

1. A widely reported interview. See, for instance, Leighton Ford, "A Tip That Can Change Your Life—but You Have to Stop and Listen," *Charlotte Observer*, May 26, 2016, accessed December 30, 2020, charlotteobserver.com/living /religion/article80030987.html. Since her death, Teresa has been canonized by the Roman Catholic Church, and is now properly referred to as Saint Teresa of Calcutta.

1. GOD'S WORD TO US

1. Philippians 1:3-4, 6, 9-11.
2. John 1:1-2.
3. Michael Casey, *Sacred Reading: The Ancient Art of* Lectio Divina (Liguori, MO: Liguori/Triumph, 1997), 44.
4. William Law, *The Power of the Spirit*, ed. Dave Hunt (Fort Washington, PA: CLC Publications, 2012), chap. 5, ebook.
5. Martin Luther, "Preface to Luther's German Writings: The Wittenberg Edition (1539)," in *The Ninety-Five Theses and Other Writings*, trans. and ed. William R. Russell (New York: Penguin, 2017), 197.
6. Sermon 7 on the Song of Songs, in Bernard of Clairvaux, *Selected Works*, trans. Gillian R. Evans (Mahwah, NJ: Paulist, 1987), 233.
7. Ezekiel 3:3.
8. Jeremiah 15:16.
9. Colossians 3:16, NRSV.
10. With insight from James Bryan Smith, *Hidden in Christ: Living as God's Beloved* (London: Hodder and Stoughton, 2014), 170. I love this thirty-day immersion in Colossians 3:1-17, a key biblical text for disciples of Christ.
11. Hebrews 4:12.

12. Origen, *Treatise on the Passover and Dialogue with Heraclides*, trans. Robert J. Daly, Ancient Christian Writers, vol. 54 (Mahwah, NJ: Paulist, 1992), 45. The injunction to "take and eat" is most notably Jesus sharing his body and blood (see Matthew 26:26), but God also told John in his vision to take and eat the scroll in Revelation 10:1-11.

13. As related in Ernest J. Fiedler, "*Lectio Divina*: Devouring God's Word," *Liturgical Ministry* 5 (1996): 69.

14. Brother Ramon, *Franciscan Spirituality: Following St. Francis Today* (London: SPCK, 1994), 114–15.

15. Ephesians 6:4, NJB.

16. Galatians 6:9, NJB.

17. 1 Corinthians 2:10-11.

18. Adaptation of John 3:16, KJV.

19. See the story in John 20:11-16. Find the article at odb.org/gB/2018/06/12/called=by=name=3.

20. Adaptation of Matthew 7:7.

21. Adaptation of Matthew 23:12.

22. Adaptation of John 14:27. I first came across this practice through the ministry of Leanne Payne.

23. God answered that prayer, although it took many more years before England fully felt like home. I write about this in *Finding Myself in Britain: Our Search for Faith, Home, and True Identity* (Milton Keynes, UK: Authentic Media, 2015).

24. Madame Guyon, "Madame Guyon: Praying the Scripture; Excerpts from Experiencing the Depths of Jesus Christ," in Richard J. Foster and James Bryan Smith, eds. *Devotional Classics: Selected Readings for Individuals and Groups*, rev. ed. (San Francisco: HarperSanFrancisco, 2005), 303.

25. Foster and Smith, *Devotional Classics*, 303.

2. LECTIO DIVINA

1. James Bryan Smith, *Hidden in Christ: Living as God's Beloved* (London: Hodder and Stoughton, 2014), 167–72.

2. Raymond Studzinski, OSB, *Reading to Live: The Evolving Practice of* Lectio Divina (Collegeville, MN: Liturgical Press, 2009), 14.

3. Jean Leclercq speaking about John of Gorze. Jean Leclercq, OSB, *The Love of Learning and the Desire for God: A Study of Monastic Culture* (New York: Fordham University Press, 1961), 73.

4. See Michael Casey, *Sacred Reading: The Ancient Art of* Lectio Divina (Liguori, MO: Liguori/Triumph, 1997), 8.

5. Dietrich Bonhoeffer, *The Way to Freedom*, trans. William Collins (New York: Harper & Row, 1966), 59.

6. Bernard of Clairvaux, *In dedicatione ecclesiae*, 5:4–5, *S. Bernardi Opera* V (Rome, 1968), 391; *Super Cantica*, 62:5, II (Rome, 1958), 158; quoted in Jean Leclercq, "*Lectio Divina*," *Worship* 58 no. 3 (1984), 248.
7. Luke 2:19.
8. See Dallas Willard, *The Divine Conspiracy: Rediscovering Our Hidden Life in God* (San Francisco: HarperSanFrancisco, 1998), 296–97.
9. Inspired by and adapted from Julia McGuinness, *Creative Praying in Groups* (London: SPCK, 2005), 91–94.

3. THE INDWELLING GOD

1. This includes Alain de Lille, a twelfth-century French poet and theologian.
2. This thought is from Thomas C. Oden, *Systematic Theology*, vol. 1, *The Living God* (Peabody, MA: Hendrickson, 2006), 67.
3. 1 Kings 8:10.
4. 1 Kings 8:27.
5. 1 Kings 9:3.
6. Isaiah 57:15.
7. Jeremiah 23:23-24.
8. Matthew 28:20.
9. Numbers 11:29.
10. Ezekiel 36:27.
11. Just a few references from Paul on union with God: 1 Corinthians 3:16, Galatians 2:20, and Colossians 1:17. For a complete listing of Paul's references and the theology behind union with God in a meaty but accessible work, see Constantine R. Campbell, *Paul and Union with Christ: An Exegetical and Theological Study* (Grand Rapids, MI: Zondervan, 2012), or for a more layperson-oriented approach, try Rankin Wilbourne, *Union with Christ: The Way to Know and Enjoy God* (Colorado Springs, CO: David C Cook, 2016).
12. See John 14–17.
13. John 15:4.
14. John Calvin was known for his thoughts on God's "condescension." For this connection to John 15, I'm indebted to Andrew Murray, *Abide in Christ* (New Kensington, PA: Whitaker House, 1979), 36.
15. John 17:21-23.
16. John 17:6-26.
17. With thanks to Bill Haley for this image, which he shared in a conversation.
18. Brother Lawrence and Frank Laubach, *Practicing His Presence* (Auburn, ME: Christian Books, 1973), 57. I rather like this approachable translation.
19. Lawrence and Laubach, *Practicing His Presence*, 47.

20. Lawrence and Laubach, *Practicing His Presence*, 55.

21. I've adapted Brother Lawrence's directions from the Frank Laubach edition of *Practicing His Presence*.

22. 1 Thessalonians 5:17.

23. John Cassian, *Conferences*, trans. Colm Luibhéid (Mahwah, NJ: Paulist, 1985), Conf. 10.10.

24. Cassian, *Conferences*, Conf. 10.10.

25. Cassian, *Conferences*, Conf. 10.10.

26. Two things to mention about Cassian. The first is that because of a controversy he encountered while in Egypt, he became vehemently opposed to imaginative prayer, which he saw not only as a great danger but even as blasphemy. The second is that he fostered a two-tiered model that elevated those living in a monastic community over laypeople. That is, he saw the goal of "Christian perfection" as available only to monks. This view contrasts with the one commonly accepted today that Christians can transform society from within, and that clergy or others in ministry aren't elevated above laypeople. If you're interested in learning more about Cassian, you can find a good one-chapter introduction in Bernard McGinn and Patricia Ferris McGinn, *Early Christian Mystics: The Divine Vision of the Spiritual Masters* (New York: Crossroad, 2003).

27. Inspired by and adapted from Julia McGuinness, *Creative Praying in Groups* (London: SPCK, 2005), 20–21.

28. Many versions are available. I used the one with a compelling foreword by James Catford: Halcyon Backhouse, ed., *The Cloud of Unknowing* (London: Hodder and Stoughton, 2009).

29. Backhouse, ed., *The Cloud of Unknowing*, 2.

4. HEARING GOD

1. You can read the story in 1 Samuel 3.

2. 1 Samuel 3:9.

3. 1 Samuel 3:19.

4. John 10:3-5.

5. Ezekiel 34:12.

6. John 10:14-15.

7. These two stories work really well when praying the Bible imaginatively—the subject of chapter 6.

8. 1 John 3:1-2.

9. I regret not knowing their names so that I could give them credit for a practice that has given back so much to me over the years. Some of the instructions for the group practice were inspired by their talks that weekend.

10. John 3:8.

11. Oswald Chambers, *My Utmost for His Highest* (UK: Oswald Chambers Publications Association, 1927; Grand Rapids, MI: Discovery House, 2017), s.v. "January 30: The Dilemma of Obedience."

12. Dallas Willard, *In Search of Guidance: Developing a Conversational Relationship with God* (San Francisco: HarperSanFrancisco, 1993), 185–86. This book was later released as *Hearing God: Developing a Conversational Relationship with God*, rev. ed. (Downers Grove, IL: IVP, 2012).

13. Willard, *In Search of Guidance*, 31.

14. Books at that time were more rare than today, although with the invention of the printing press in 1440, they were more readily available than when they were created by hand.

15. Teresa of Ávila, *The Book of Her Life*, in Kieran Kavanaugh and Otilio Rodriguez, trans., *The Collected Works of Saint Teresa of Ávila*, vol. 1 (Washington, DC: ICS Publications, 1976), chap. 25, sec. 6.

16. Teresa of Ávila, *The Interior Castle*, in Kieran Kavanaugh and Otilio Rodriguez, trans., *The Collected Works of Saint Teresa of Ávila*, vol. 2 (Washington, DC: ICS Publications, 1980), pt. IV, chap. 3, sec. 4.

17. Teresa of Ávila, *Interior Castle*, pt. IV, chap. 3, sec. 4.

18. Teresa of Ávila, *Interior Castle*, pt. VI, chap 3, sec. 13.

19. Teresa of Ávila, *Interior Castle*, pt. VI, chap. 3, sec. 15.

20. Teresa of Ávila, *Interior Castle*, pt. VI, chap. 3, sec. 18.

21. Teresa of Ávila, *Interior Castle*, pt. VI, chap. 3, sec. 16.

22. Teresa of Ávila, *Interior Castle*, pt. VI, chap. 3, sec. 4.

23. Teresa of Ávila, *Interior Castle*, pt. VI, chap. 3, sec. 6.

24. Teresa of Ávila, *Interior Castle*, pt. VI, chap. 3, sec. 8.

25. Teresa of Ávila, *Interior Castle*, pt. VI, chap. 3, sec. 17.

26. Teresa of Ávila, *The Way of Perfection*, trans. and ed. E. Allison Peers (New York: Image Books, 1964), accessed August 3, 2019, catholicplanet.com /ebooks/Way-of-Perfection.pdf.

27. Prayers have been updated and adapted from *The Way of Perfection* (based on the Peers translation, which is in the public domain).

28. Teresa of Ávila, *The Way of Perfection*, 86.

29. Teresa of Ávila, *The Way of Perfection*, 128.

30. Teresa of Ávila, *The Way of Perfection*, 84.

31. Teresa of Ávila, *The Way of Perfection*, 59.

32. Teresa of Ávila, *The Way of Perfection*, 76–77.

5. THE PRAYER OF LAMENT

1. Depending on how you count them, there are sixty-seven psalms of lament. See J. Todd Billings, *Rejoicing in Lament: Wrestling with Incurable Cancer and Life in Christ* (Grand Rapids, MI: Brazos, 2015), 12.
2. Psalm 13:1.
3. Psalm 13:5.
4. Psalm 22:1.
5. Psalm 22:1-2, 15.
6. Paraphrase of Psalm 22:3-5.
7. Psalm 22:19-21.
8. Psalm 22:9, 22, 24, 27, 31.
9. Psalm 22:22, emphasis added.
10. Job 19:25-27.
11. The idea I've engaged with of writing out a permission slip is from Tanya Marlow, who includes it regularly in her *Thorns and Gold* newsletter. See tanyamarlow.com.
12. In mentioning this work, I should note that I'm not recommending much of the theology it expresses, for the views are not Trinitarian but dip into a folk legend based on a deification of Mary. Yet as Christians we can engage with works that make us think critically about what we believe while weighing what we agree with and what we don't.
13. Sue Monk Kidd, *The Secret Life of Bees* (New York: Penguin, 2003), 97.
14. This prayer exercise was partly inspired by "Bitter, Sweet, Salt, and Sour" in Sue Wallace, *Multi-Sensory Worship* (Bletchley, UK: Scripture Union, 2009), 58; and "An Abridged Passover Haggadah in English" in Michele Guinness, *The Heavenly Party* (Oxford: Monarch Books, 2007), 251–82. I highly recommend Michele's book, including the full instructions of how to host a Passover meal. We've enjoyed doing this in our church.
15. Numbers 28:2.
16. Ephesians 5:2.
17. Exodus 3:8.

6. ENTERING THE STORY

1. Ignatius had been reading *The Life of Christ* by Ludolph of Saxony from the fourteenth century, and *The Golden Legend*, a book on the lives of the saints compiled in the thirteenth century by Jacopo of Varazze. He wasn't the first to pray this way. For instance, Francis of Assisi encouraged people to create Nativity scenes so they could imagine Mary, Joseph, and Jesus as people just like we are.

2. "From mystery to history, from history to mystery—pressing ever towards the full, rich experience of mystery in history, history as mystery." Joseph P. Whelan, "Jesuit Apostolic Prayer" in *The Way Supplement* 19 (1973), 17.

3. I was following the first contemplation in the second week of *The Spiritual Exercises*. See Joseph A. Munitiz and Philip Endean, trans., *Saint Ignatius of Loyola: Personal Writings* (London: Penguin, 2004), 305–6.

4. Some of this material is adapted from "Praying Scripture with the Imagination," day 8 of "31 Days of St. Ignatius 2018," *Pathways to God*, accessed September 21, 2018, pathwaystogod.org/day-8-31-days-st-ignatius -2018; "How Do We Pray with Our Imagination?," Collaborative Ministry Office, Creighton University, accessed March 26, 2019, onlineministries .creighton.edu/CollaborativeMinistry/Imagination/Intro.html; and Jeannie Oestreicher and Larry Warner, *Imaginative Prayer for Youth Ministry: A Guide to Transforming Your Students' Spiritual Lives into Journey, Adventure, and Encounter* (Grand Rapids, MI: Zondervan, 2006).

5. To experience their writing, see Tanya Marlow, *Those Who Wait: Finding God in Disappointment, Doubt, and Delay* (UK: Malcolm Down Publishing, 2017), and Amy Scott Robinson, *Image of the Invisible: Daily Bible Readings from Advent to Epiphany* (Abingdon, UK: BRF, 2019).

6. I recommend the 1996 Penguin version of Ignatius's *Spiritual Exercises*, which lists the fifty gospel stories on pages 334–48. If you don't have a copy, you can also find a 1914 translation online: *The Spiritual Exercises of St. Ignatius of Loyola*, trans. Father Elder Mullan (New York: P. J. Kennedy & Sons, 1914), documentacatholicaomnia.eu/03d/1491-1556,_Ignatius_Loyola, _Spiritual_Exercises,_EN.pdf.

7. REMEMBERING IN PRAYER

1. David L. Fleming, S.J., "Finding a Busy God" in *A Spirituality for Contemporary Life: The Jesuit Heritage Today*, ed. David L. Fleming, S.J., (St. Louis: Review for Religious, 1991), 21, quoted in Joseph A. Tetlow, S.J., "The Most Postmodern Prayer: American Jesuit Identity and the Examen of Conscience, 1920–1990," *Studies in the Spirituality of Jesuits* 26, no. 1 (1994), 16.

2. Hugh Kelly, "St. Ignatius and the Spiritual Exercises," *Studies: An Irish Quarterly Review* 45, no. 179 (Autumn 1956): 279.

3. See George A. Aschenbrenner, S.J., "Consciousness Examen: Becoming God's Heart for the World," *Review for Religious* 47, no. 6 (November/ December 1988): 801–10, nebula.wsimg.com/ff34f72609386a53fd0e827 9707b1763?AccessKeyId=BEEADDF369000DCF3CC9&disposition=0 &alloworigin=1.

4. Mark Argent, "Reclaiming the Particular Examen," *The Way* 52, no. 4 (October 2013): 60.

5. Saint Ignatius of Loyola, "To Father Simão Rodrigues: On Being a Reconciler" (Rome, March 18, 1542), Woodstock Theological Library at Georgetown University, accessed January 14, 2021, library.georgetown.edu /woodstock/ignatius-letters/letter2#letter.

6. Forgiveness is a key way to pray. I've written a through-the-Bible look at forgiveness in forty-plus daily devotionals. See *The Living Cross: Exploring God's Gift of Forgiveness and New Life* (Abingdon, UK: BRF, 2016).

7. See, for instance, Colossians 3 or Ephesians 4:22-24. In Paul's letter to the believers in Ephesus, the Greek verb clauses "to put off your old self," "to be made new," and "to put on the new self" indicate a continuous action.

8. See Philippians 2:5 and Galatians 5:22-23.

9. I have drawn in this section from Aschenbrenner, "Consciousness Examen," *Review for Religious*, 804–8.

10. A wonderful book of thirty-four examens that focus on one area each is Mark Thibodeaux's *Reimagining the Ignatian Examen: Fresh Ways to Pray from Your Day* (Chicago: Loyola Press, 2015). You can also find his content in an abbreviated form on a daily app under the same name.

11. The first four sets of two-pronged questions are inspired by a delightful picture book for adults: Dennis Linn, Sheila Fabricant Linn, and Matthew Linn, *Sleeping with Bread: Holding What Gives You Life* (Mahwah, NJ: Paulist, 1995), 6–7.

12. These are the main questions Cindy Bunch asks in her approachable book on living out the examen: *Be Kind to Yourself: Releasing Frustrations and Embracing Joy* (Downers Grove, IL: IVP, 2020).

13. This exercise was inspired by "A Particular Relationship," examen 4 in Mark Thibodeaux, S.J., *Reimagining the Ignatian Examen*, 11–13.

14. See "John Wesley and the Holy Club's 22 Questions," Hope, Faith, Prayer, accessed June 2, 2017, hopefaithprayer.com/john-wesley-holy -club-questions/.

AFTERWORD

1. Mark 9:29. I'm taking this slightly out of context, as I'm not referring to a demon.

2. Louis Evely, *That Man Is You*, trans. Edmond Bonin (New York: Paulist, 1964), 16–17.

THE NAVIGATORS® STORY

T HANK YOU for picking up this NavPress book! We hope it has been a blessing to you.

NavPress is a ministry of The Navigators. The Navigators began in the 1930s, when a young California lumberyard worker named Dawson Trotman was impacted by basic discipleship principles and felt called to teach those principles to others. He saw this mission as an echo of 2 Timothy 2:2: "And the things you have heard me say in the presence of many witnesses entrust to reliable people who will also be qualified to teach others" (NIV).

In 1933, Trotman and his friends began discipling members of the US Navy. By the end of World War II, thousands of men on ships and bases around the world were learning the principles of spiritual multiplication by the intentional, person-to-person teaching of God's Word.

After World War II, The Navigators expanded its relational ministry to include college campuses; local churches; the Glen Eyrie Conference Center and Eagle Lake Camps in Colorado Springs, Colorado; and neighborhood and citywide initiatives across the country and around the world.

Today, with more than 2,600 US staff members—and local ministries in more than 100 countries—The Navigators continues the transformational process of making disciples who make more disciples, advancing the Kingdom of God in a world that desperately needs the hope and salvation of Jesus Christ and the encouragement to grow deeper in relationship with Him.

NavPress was created in 1975 to advance the calling of The Navigators by bringing biblically rooted and culturally relevant products to people who want to know and love Christ more deeply. In January 2014, NavPress entered an alliance with Tyndale House Publishers to strengthen and better position our rich content for the future. Through *THE MESSAGE* Bible and other resources, NavPress seeks to bring positive spiritual movement to people's lives.

If you're interested in learning more or becoming involved with The Navigators, go to navigators.org. For more discipleship content from The Navigators and NavPress authors, visit thedisciplemaker.org. May God bless you in your walk with Him!

navpress.com

CP1308